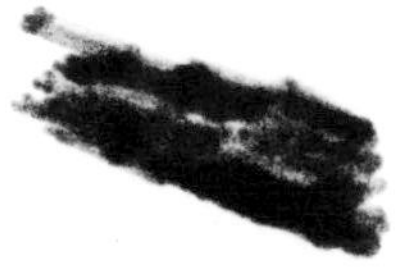

Guide to the New England Irish 3rd Edition

Michael P. Quinlin and Colette Minogue Quinlin

Quinlin Campbell Publishers
Boston

Published by Quinlin Campbell Publishers
PO Box 651, Boston, MA 02134
Tel/Fax: (617) 825-1404

Cover design by Joan Ross and Jim Higgins, Higgins & Ross Photography & Design

Interior design by Leslie Anne Feagley

ISBN #0-934665-11-7
First Printing June 1994

To the memory of
Catherine Minogue,
Thomas Flannan Minogue
and
John J. Quinlin

ACKNOWLEDGMENTS

The Guide to the New England Irish was made possible by the friendship, support and dedication of the following people:

Leslie Anne Feagley, Jim Higgins, Joan Ross, Dan Mazik and Vernice Kelly for their unfailing imagination, patience and production expertise;

Alan Loughnane, Paul O'Neil, Jim Gallagher, Mance Grady, Mick Griffin, Maureen Doherty, John Curran, Kevin Mulligan, Dave Burke, Larry Reynolds and Seamus Connolly for identifying and supplying the missing pieces.

Thanks to Jim Ford, scholar and gentleman, who originated the idea of a Boston Irish Heritage Trail, and whose excellent Walking Tours of Irish Sites provides an in-depth treatment. Also thanks to Kathy Kottaridis, Chuck O'Connell, Henry Lee and Justine Liff for insights and feedback.

Thanks to the advertisers for supporting this project.

Thanks to Margaret Quinlin for her expert advice, insight and encouragement.

Finally, special thanks to Master Leo McLoughlin, Chief Office Boy and envelope stuffer.

Table of Contents

Connecticut

Maine

Massachusetts

New Hampshire

Rhode Island

Vermont

Introduction

When Mary Robinson, President of Ireland, visited Boston in March 1994, she met with Irish from all walks of life, from dignitaries, scholars and business leaders to newly-arrived immigrants eager to forge ahead in their adopted country. As a former immigrant to New England herself, President Robinson was impressed by the extensive networks in place both for the new Irish and for Irish-Americans intent upon learning about Irish history and culture.

The **Guide to the New England Irish,** third edition, has pieced together the networks established by the new Irish, previous generations of immigrants and Irish-Americans. The result is a directory of over 1,200 Irish businesses, services, and cultural groups ranging from gift shops, pubs and restaurants and social clubs to language courses, theater groups and immigration centers. We especially hope you'll be pleased to discover so many education courses, philanthropic programs and cultural activities flourishing in the Irish-American community.

The Irish have been coming to New England since the 17th century, as names like Belfast, Maine and Dublin, New Hampshire clearly indicate. They have settled here and assimilated as Americans, while keeping a keen interest in their Irish heritage. That is why you'll see so many Americans eager to learn the Irish language, or taking up the tin whistle or fiddle in places like Nashua, Providence, Portland, Burlington and Hartford.

Irish-American interest in Irish culture has been enhanced over the past ten years by the most recent cycle of immigration, as tens of thousands of Irish people arrive here seeking opportunities. Thanks to two New Englanders, Brian Donnelly of Massachusetts and Bruce Morrison of Connecticut, who as U.S. Congressmen helped amend U.S. immigration policies, many of the new Irish obtained visas which enabled them to settle and prosper here.

According to the 1990 U.S. Census, nearly 3 million New Englanders consider themselves of Irish ancestry. That's over 20% of the population, or one in five people. The **Guide** is divided by state, and in the frontpiece of each section you'll see a breakdown of Irish-Americans for that state. We're fairly sure these numbers do not include the thousands of Irish who were undocumented when the Census was taken, and we believe the Census in the year 2,000 will more accurately reflect the new generation of Irish who have settled in New England.

The information in the **Guide** will help the Irish community in New England stay abreast of various activities throughout the region. It will also be of value to visitors from outside New England who want to experience the wealth of Irish-American culture found here. Traditional music sessions, hand-made Irish goods, Irish theater, and authentic Irish restaurants and pubs are all immediately accessible to intrepid visitors as well as to local residents. The **Guide to the New England Irish** is the only publication on the market to capture this information under one cover.

Finally, we have been diligent in pursuing all facets of the Irish and Irish-American communities through advertising and mailings, but if you were somehow omitted from the third edition of the **Guide to the New England Irish,** please write or call for a questionnaire which will insure your inclusion and free listing in the 1996 edition.

Michael P. Quinlin and Colette Minogue Quinlin
Boston, MA
June 1994

Connecticut's population: 3,287,116
Connecticut's Irish population: 613,924

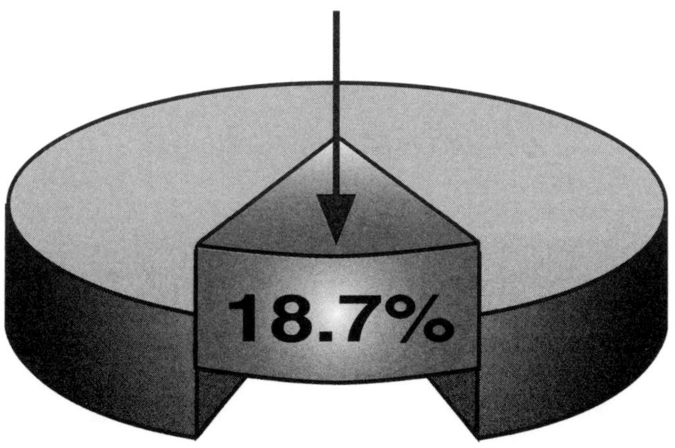

Annual Events

FEISEANNA

For Feis information or to register a Feis, write to: Mrs. Patricia Dwyer, President, North American Feis Commission (NAFC), 17 Lillburn Drive, Stony Point, New York 10980.

February
Shamrock School Feis
Contact: Sheila Stevens
(203) 225-0671

March
Griffith Academy Feis
Contact: Colleen Griffith
(203) 258-4048

April
Connecticut State Feis
Contact: John O'Keefe
(203) 865-7542

April
Horgan Academy Feis
Contact: Maureen Horgan
(203) 723-0568

May
Western Connecticut State Feis
Contact: Iris Gray Sharnick
(203) 743-7001

June
The Hartford Feis
Contact: John Droney
(203) 521-2696

June
New Haven Feis
Contact: Madge Mulhall
(203) 268-2037

July
Stamford AOH Annual Feis
Contact: Maura O'Connell
(203) 325-3172

August
The New London AOH Feis
Contact: James Gallagher
(203) 739-8216

October
Fall Foliage Feis
Contact: Jack McArdle
(203) 485-0027

October
Horgan Academy Feis
Contact: Maureen Horgan
(203) 723-0568

FESTIVALS

Connecticut Irish Festival
Yale Field, Route 34
New Haven, CT
Contact: John Lawless
(203) 469-3080
This annual event is sponsored by the Irish-American Community Center and The New Haven Gaelic Football and Hurling Club. Featuring music, dance and competitions in language, singing, arts and crafts and Irish bread making. Athletic events include football, hurling, rugby and soccer. Admission is $6.00 per day for adults or $12.00 for a three day pass. Children admitted free. Held the fourth weekend in June.

Fairfield Irish Festival
Roger Ludlowe Field
Unquowa Road
Fairfield, CT 06430
(203) 255-8134
Sponsored by Féile, Inc., which is affiliated with the Gaelic-American Cultural Center. This three day festival features dozens of top showbands and traditional Irish musicians. Admission is $6.00 per day or $12.00 for a three day pass. Children under 16 are free if accompanied by an adult. Held over Father's Day weekend in June.

Greater Hartford Irish Festival
132 Commerce Street
Glastonbury, CT
(203) 633-9691
Held the last weekend in July.

OTHER

Bloomsday Celebration
PO Box 11088
Greenwich, CT 06831
Contact: Tom Toohy
(203) 531-5547
Sponsored by the Wild Geese Society to celebrate the legendary Irish author, James Joyce. Held in June.

PARADES

Bridgeport Parade
Contact: Margaret Dzunko
(203) 378-9252

Greenwich Parade
Contact: The Hibernian Society
Held the Sunday before St. Patrick's Day.

Hartford Parade
Contact: Irish-American Home Society
(203) 633-9691
Held the Saturday before St. Patrick's Day.

Meriden Parade
Contact: Frank Kearney
(203) 235-2746
Held the Saturday following St. Patrick's Day.

New Haven Parade
Contact: St. Patrick's Day Committee
PO Box 186
New Haven, CT 06513
Held the Sunday before St. Patrick's Day.

Artisans

CELTIC ART/ART

Claddagh Carver
46 Jodi Drive
Wallingford, CT 06492
Contact: Jim Sheehan
(203) 265-2473

Barbara Hayden
136 Compo Road
Westport, CT 06880
(203) 227-2925

Tom McAndrew
7 Whippoorwill Road
Old Lyme, CT
(203) 434-5531

Rannock Moor
c/o Julie Vecchio
266 Thimble Island Road
Branford, CT 06405
(203) 483-5282

Ann Samul
15 Pacific Street
New London, CT 06320
(203) 442-5695

Teernahilan Irish Art
26 Francis Street
Norwalk, CT 06851
Contact: Kevin Callahan
(203) 846-1881 1-800-548-8619

Handmade Arts & Crafts

Heraldry
37 Westbrook Road
West Hartford, CT 06107
Contact: Patrick Mangan
(203) 561-1862
Makers of heraldic shields showing family coat-of-arms in full color on copper stampings. Shields in mahogany in three sizes, small (10" x 7"), large (10" x 14") and double (11" x 11").

Storytelling

The Shanachies of Connecticut
Contact: Jeanne Hickey
(203) 468-0426
The history of the Connecticut-Irish through storytelling and ballads.

Theater

Clan na Gael Players
The Gaelic-American Club Féile
1494 Post Road
Fairfield, CT 06430
Contact: Peg O'Leary
(203) 261-4944
Irish plays, staged readings and poetry recitations. Performances at festivals, willing to travel.

New Haven Gaelic Players
1032 North Main Street
Wallingford, CT 06492
Contact: Charles Starrs
(203) 265-2957
Annual production in the fall, spring workshop and summer festival.

Education

Colleges & Universities

Central Connecticut State College
New Britain, CT 06050
Contact: John Conway
(203) 827-7556 - English Dept.
Undergraduate courses in modern Irish literature, Joyce, and Yeats, and a graduate course on Yeats. The Library acquired The Bell literary journal on microfiche.

Connecticut College
New London, CT 06320
(203) 439-2350 - English Dept.
Undergraduate courses on Yeats and Joyce.

Fairfield University
Fairfield, CT 06430
Contact: Dianne Menagh
(203) 254-4000 - English Dept.
Undergraduate courses in Irish literature, Joyce, and American immigrant history.

Hartford College for Women
Hartford, CT 06106
Contact: Lawrence Scanlon
Irish literature courses.

Mohegan College
Norwich, CT 06360
Contact: John McLean
(203) 886-1931 Ext. 201
Exchange program at St. Patrick's College, Maynooth, and summer programs at Trinity College, Dublin.

Quinnipiac College
Hamden, CT 06518
Contact: Dennis Cashman
(203) 288-5251 - History Dept.
Undergraduate courses in politics and religion on modern Ireland. Courses are also available on a non-credit basis.

Sacred Heart University
Bridgeport, CT 06606
Contact: Walter Brooks
(203) 371-7730 - Religious Studies Dept.
Offers a study abroad program at Trinity College, Dublin.

Southern Connecticut State College
New Haven, CT 06511
Contact: Professor Sandomirsky
(203) 397-4000
Courses in Celtic mythology.

St. Joseph's College
West Hartford, CT 06117
(203) 232-4571 - English Dept.
Undergraduate courses on Joyce, Yeats, Synge, and the Irish Drama Movement.

Trinity College
Hartford, CT 06106
Contact: James Wheatley
(203) 297-2000 - English Dept.
Undergraduate courses in modern Irish literature, including Joyce and Yeats.

University of Connecticut
Groton, CT
Contact: Steven Jones
(203) 446-1020
Undergraduate and graduate courses in Irish literature.

University of Connecticut
Hartford, CT
Contact: Thomas Shea
(203) 241-4832
Undergraduate and graduate courses in Irish literature.

University of Connecticut
Storrs, CT 06268
Contact: Lee Jacobus
(203) 486-2570 - English Dept.
Undergraduate and graduate courses in Irish literature.

University of Connecticut
Waterbury, CT
Contact: Rachel Lynch
(203) 596-4080
Undergraduate and graduate courses in Irish literature.

University of Hartford
West Hartford, CT 06117
Contact: Thomas Smith
(203) 768-4100 - English Dept.
Undergraduate courses in Irish literature.

Wesleyan University
Middlestown, CT 06457
Contact: Alfred Turko
(203) 347-9411 - English Dept.
Course available in Irish theater.

Western Connecticut State College
Danbury, CT 06810
Contact: Edward Hagen
(203) 837-9041 - English Dept.
Graduate and undergraduate courses in Irish literature and James Joyce.

Yale University
New Haven, CT 06520
Contact: Jonathan Spence
(203) 436-1282 - History Dept.
Undergraduate courses in Irish literature and graduate courses in Irish history.

Language Classes

Jim Fahey
Fairfield, CT
(203) 255-5845

Ray Greene
104 Commonwealth Avenue
New Britain, CT 06053
(203) 224-2269

Joan Kennedy
41 Peck Road
Bethany, CT 06525
(203) 393-0377

David Manning
Oxford, CT
(203) 888-4041

Elaine Murphy Chicoine
47 Quaddick Road
Thompson, CT 06277
(203) 923-2883

Library Collections

Connecticut Irish-American Historical Society
c/o The Irish-American
Community Center
Venice Place
East Haven, CT 06512
(203) 469-3080
A collection of Irish history with a concentration on the Connecticut-Irish.

Fairfield University Library
Fairfield, CT 06430
(203) 254-4044
Fairfield University Library houses a facsimile of The Book of Kells. Presented by the Wild Geese Society.

Sacred Heart University Library
Bridgeport, CT 06606
(203) 371-7700
This library contains collections of Irish history and literature.

Sterling Memorial Library
Yale University
New Haven, CT 06520
(203) 432-1775
Sterling Memorial Library houses the Garvan Collection, an excellent collection of Irish literature, including manuscripts, some uncatalogued. It also has papers on Edmund Burke.

Museums

Nautilus Museum
Navy Submarine Base
Route 12
Groton, CT
(203) 445-3174
The museum contains an exhibit of the world's first submarine which was invented by John P. Holland, a Clare native, who christened it "The Fenian."

Music/Dance

Bands & Performers

Barley Bree
Post Office Box 8207
Manchester, CT 06040
Contact: P. V. O'Donnell
(203) 645-8404
Hailing from Counties Donegal and Tyrone, Barley Bree has been performing Irish folk and traditional music along with stories for almost 20 years.

Bold Fenian Men
3 Patriot Ridge Road
Sandyhook, CT 06482
Contact: Tommy Sheehan
(203) 426-8535

Tom Callinan
168 Shore Road
Clinton, CT 06413
(203) 669-6648

Celtic DJ
PO Box 94
Waterford, CT 06385
(203) 442-7197

Comhaltas Ceoltóirí Éireann
Curry-Seery Branch
41 Peck Road
Bethany, CT 06525
Contact: Joan Kennedy
(203) 393-0377
Preserves and promotes traditional Irish music and dance statewide. Coordinates adult ceili and set-dance lessons. Holds monthly ceili's at various locations across the state and also coordinates an annual concert.

Joe Gerhard
92 Livingston Street
New Haven, CT 06511
Fiddle and guitar.

Green Briar Ceili Band
(203) 261-8096

Skip Healey
c/o Empty Pockets Productions
PO Box 854
East Greenwich, RI 02818
Flute and whistle. Album entitled "Farewell New England Shores."

Brendan McCann
(203) 327-4177
Accordion.

Michael (Skip) McKinley
145 Water Street
Stonington, CT 06378
(203) 535-2342 Fax: (203) 535-2342
Traditional flute player with a recently released album entitled "The Executive Session."

Josephine McNamara
(203) 327-4177
Singer.

Becky Miller
36 Brainerd Avenue
Middletown, CT 06457
(203) 347-2343

John Moran
238 Maple Tree Hill Road
Oxford, CT 06483
(203) 264-0178
Singer.

Morrison Visa
c/o Irish-American Home Society
Glastonbury, CT 06033

Music in the Glen Ceili Band
West Haven, CT
Contact: Joe Heeran
(203) 265-2925
Traditional and Ceili music in the New Haven area. They also play at the Friday night Ceili at the Hibernian Hall in Stamford.

The Ould Sod
Kensington, CT
Contact: Thomas Walsh
(203) 828-5902
Ballads, pub songs and old time dances performed by Terry Clen and Thomas Walsh.

Dave Paton
(203) 364-5661
Concertina.

Patrick Speer
50 Goddard Avenue
Bridgeport, CT 06610
(203) 333-4544

John Tabb
47 Cricket Lane
Somers, CT 06071
(203) 749-9098

John Whalan
(203) 968-1440
Accordion.

Dancing Adjudicators

Iris Gray Sharnick
11 Willow Brook Lane
Newton, CT 06470
(203) 426-1634

Patricia Lenihan
25 Crestwood Road
Monroe, CT 06468
(203) 261-6656

Mary Robinson
304 Stanley Street
Monroe, CT 06468
(203) 268-4497

Sheila Stevens
29 Liberty Street
New Britain, CT 06502
(203) 225-0671

Mary Whelan Duffy
24 Carroll Road
East Hartford, CT 06108
(203) 528-3273

Anna Mae Zachorewitz
31 Marmor Court
Wethersfield, CT 06109
(203) 529-2369

Dancing Groups

Stamford Ceili Group
Contact: Sharon McGovern
(203) 268-1852
Friday evening ceili's at the Hibernian Hall, 43 forest Street, Stamford.

Dancing Teachers

Ann Devine
264 Deer Run Trail
Manchester, CT 06040
(203) 649-4553

Deirdre Golden Davies
66 Brandy Street
Bolton, CT 06043
(203) 643-5699

Maura Ann Gray
97 Mill Ridge Road
Danbury, CT 06810
(203) 743-7001

Iris Gray Sharnick
PO Box 3494
Danbury, CT 06813
(203) 743-7001

Mary Beth Griffith
140 Ox Yoke Drive
Wethersfield, CT 06109
(203) 258-4048

Irene Horgan
471 N. Main Street
Naugatuck, CT 06770
(203) 723-0568

Maureen Anne Horgan
Post Office Box 1415
Naugatuck, CT 06770
(203) 723-8767

Patricia Lenihan
25 Crestwood Road
Monroe, CT 06468
(203) 261-6656

John Lydon
50 Crystal Street
New Canaan, CT 06840
(203) 966-3885

Kathleen Mulkerin
20 Leonard Street
West Haven, CT 06516
(203) 934-2267

Julie O'Connell
76 Treat Street
Stamford, CT 06906
(203) 323-7578

Johanna O'Connell Reilly
95 Wadsworth Lane
Willimantic, CT 06226
(203) 423-8700

John Patrick O'Keefe
193 Dover Street
New Haven, CT 06513
(203) 865-7542

Nancy Redden
11 Crestview Road
Tariffville, CT 06081
(203) 651-4677

Joyce Oliphant Shea
96 Plank Road
Prospect, CT 06712
(203) 758-6266

Sheila Stevens
29 Liberty Street
New Britain, CT 06052
(203) 225-2137

Mary Whelan Duffy
24 Carroll Road
East Hartford, CT 06108
(203) 528-3273

Saturday:
ADRIAN FLANNELLY SHOW
11:00 am - 1.00 pm

Current Events, Interviews
Arts & Entertainment,
"Budweiser Bulletin Board" Segment
News & Sports
Live-Link with *MWR & NWR Radio*
simulcasting in Counties:
Clare, Mayo, Galway, Sligo, Leitrim, Roscommon, Longford, Cavan, Fermanagh, Tyrone, Donegal and Derry.

Sunday:
FLANNELLY SUNDAY SHOW
8.30 pm - 10.00 pm

News & Sports from Ireland
"Budweiser Bulletin Board" Segment
Music, Music, Music, Music

- Public Relations
- Advertising
- Entertainment
- Sales Promotion

515 Madison Avenue • Suite 1120 • New York, New York 10022
212/935-0606 • Fax: 212/593-2111

Music Promoters

Ninnau Welsh Talent Agency
10 Hemingway Road
North Haven, CT 06473
(203) 239-1410
Represents the Celtic tradition of Wales, including folk groups, choirs, poets and harpists. Distributes Sain Records of Wales.

Radio Programs

WGCH 1450 AM
"Irish Hour"
Sunday evenings
Contact: Noel McGovern
(203) 268-1852

WNHU 87.9 FM
"Echoes of Erin"
6:00 p.m. to 8:00 p.m. on Tuesdays
Contact: John O'Donovan/
Joan Kennedy/Pat Kennedy
(203) 934-9296

WNHU 87.9 FM
"Echoes of Erin"
6:30 p.m. to 8:00 p.m. on Thursdays
Contact: Tom Faherty
(203) 934-9296

WNTY 990 AM
"Music of Erin"
Wallingford, CT
10:00 a.m. to 11:00 a.m. on Saturdays
Contact: Peter Guinan/P. J. Tierney
(203) 294-1443

WPKN 89.5 FM
"Thistle and Shamrock"
10:00 p.m. to 11:00 p.m. on Saturdays
Contact: Fiona Ritchie (Syndicated)
(704) 549-9323

WVOF 88.5 FM
"Celtic Heritage"
11:00 a.m. to 1:00 p.m. on Sundays
Contact: Barbara Hayden/
Peg O'Connor/Jim Sullivan
(203) 227-2925

WYBC 93.3 FM
"Sound of Ireland"
West Haven, CT
9:00 p.m. to 11:00 p.m. on Sundays
Contact: Sean Canning
(203) 432-9433

Tapes & CD's

The Executive Session
145 Water Street
Stonington, CT 06378
Contact: Michael (Skip) McKinley
(203) 535-2342 Fax: (203) 535-2342
Traditional flute player with a recently released album entitled "The Executive Session."

Green Linnet Records
43 Beaver Brook Road
Danbury, CT 06810
Contact: Chris Teskey
(203) 730-0333 Fax: (203) 730-0345
Celtic and world music labels with over 200 titles on catalog, including recordings by Altan, De Dannan, The Bothy Band and Kevin Burke.

Oenoke Records, Inc.
646 Rockrimmon Road
Stamford, CT 06903
Contact: John Whalan
(203) 968-1440

Television

Greater New Haven Celtic Television Association
Contact: Thomas Gallagher
(203) 932-2255

Organizations

Businesses/ Investments

Irish Chamber of Commerce in the USA, Inc. (ICCUSA)
1305 Post Road, Suite 205
Fairfield, CT 06430
Contact: Charles Boyle
(203) 255-4774 Fax: (203) 255-6752
Executive network representing over 300 US and Irish companies. Conducts the Annual Trade Mission to Ireland in May/June. Provides a complete library of information on doing business between the US and Ireland. Call (203) 877-8131 from your facsimile/phone to access library.

Northern Ireland Partnership
18 Cutler Street
Stonington, CT 06378
Contact: Michael Blair
(203) 535-0236
(203) 535-4291 (fax)

Telecom Éireann U.S. Ltd.
6 Landmark Square
Stamford, CT
Contact: Shay Flarin
(203) 359-5659
(203) 359-5849 (fax)
Provides telecommunication systems, including telephones, mobile systems and broadcasting.

History & Cultural Societies

Connecticut Irish Heritage Council
PO Box 682
New London, CT 06320
Contact: James Gallagher
(203) 739-8216
Contact: Neil Hogan
(203) 269-9154
A statewide coordinating body to promote and preserve Irish history and culture and to improve communications among Irish-American people through clubs, education, music, theater and the arts.

Irish-American Historical Society of Connecticut
Box 120-020
East Haven, CT 06512
Contact: Jeanne Hickey
(203) 468-0426
Dedicated to preserving all available records of the Irish in America, collecting interviews of the Connecticut-Irish, providing quality programs, publishing a Shanachie Newsletter, and disseminating information with other Irish-American groups.

Wild Geese Society
Box 11088
Greenwich, CT 06832
Contact: Tom Toohy
(203) 531-5547
Sponsors a regular series of cultural programs, an annual Irish language week, film festivals and newsletters.

PHILANTHROPY

AOH Irish Way Scholarship
98 Hall Avenue, #91
Meridan, CT 06450
Contact: Frank Kearney
(203) 235-2746

International Irish Scholarship Committee
75 Johnson Street
Trumbull, CT 06611
Contact: Bob Sheehan
(203) 268-5109

John F. Kennedy Trust
c/o Robert Donahue
One Financial Plaza
Hartford, CT 06103
(203) 947-6501
(203) 527-0143 (fax)
To benefit the Kennedy Centre, New Ross, County Wexford, Ireland.

Project Children
95 Bartlett Drive
Madison, CT 06443
Contact: Peter McLaughlin
(203) 421-3122
A national program to benefit Catholic and Protestant children from Northern Ireland who visit the US for a summer away from strife.

St. Bridgid's Scholarship Committee
501 Pilgrims Harbor
Wallingford, CT 06492
Contact: Cathy Brannelly Austin
Adult women's literacy.

CONNECTICUT

St. Patrick's Scholarship Committee
438 Wakely Avenue
Stratford, CT 06497

Wild Geese Society
Box 11088
Greenwich, CT 06831
Contact: Tom Toohy
(203) 531-5547
Sponsors a regular series of cultural programs, an annual Irish language week, film festivals and newsletters. Also supports Project Children and Irish Way Scholarships.

Political/ Human Rights Clubs

American-Irish Political Education Committee
21 Pierce Lane
Madison, CT 06443
Contact: Frank O'Day
(203) 245-4739

AOH Political Education Committee
351 Boston Post Road
East Lyme, CT 06333
Contact: Jim Gallagher
(207) 739-8219

Irish-American Unity Conference
16 Forest View Street
Trumbull, CT 06111
Contact: Maurice Kiely
(203) 372-3938

Irish Northern Aid
30 Russ Street
Hartford, CT 06106
Contact: Richard Lawlor, Esq.
(203) 549-3750
INA is the oldest and largest organization in the US, dedicated exclusively to aiding the Nationalist victims of the Anglo-Irish conflict. The families of nearly 1,000 prisoners in five countries rely upon the dedication of volunteers to fund-raise across America on behalf of An Cuman Cabhrach and Green Cross, prisoner assisted trusts based in Ireland since the 1950's. INA works with Irish-Americans and human and civil rights groups to promote an end to conflict, to aid the release of prisoners, and to end British occupation of six counties in Ireland.

Social Clubs

Ancient Order of Hibernians
The AOH was organized on May 4, 1836 in New York City. It played a pivotal role in helping Irish immigrants adjust to American society during the 19th century. Today the men's and women's branches of the AOH are active across the country promoting Irish culture, contributing to American values, Christian charity, the Catholic Church, supporting issues in Ireland and Northern Ireland and promoting friendship and unity within the organization. The Connecticut divisions are as follows:

State President
Thomas Egan
8 Maple Drive
Sandy Hook, CT 06482
(203) 426-5136

Garry Barrows
24 Spicer Avenue
Groton, CT 06340
(203) 446-1325

Paul Butler
49 Marlene Street
Bristol, CT 06010
(203) 589-5462

John Cooney, Jr.
9 Sunset Terrace
Portland, CT 06480
(203) 342-1690

James Curran
14 Marshall Avenue
Naugatuck, CT 06770
(203) 729-2620

Jerry Curran
32 North Street
Ridgefield, CT 06877
(203) 438-0776

Timothy Dillon
24 Elderberry Lane
Shelton, CT 06484
(203) 734-2591

Francis Doolan
34 Woodtick Road
Wolcot, CT 06716
(203) 879-1002

ORGANIZATIONS

James Finley, Jr.
6 Banta Lane
Durham, CT 06422
(203) 349-0844

Dan Foley
85 Highridge Avenue
South Windsor, CT 06074

Robert Hemming
24 East Brown Street
West Haven, CT 06516
(203) 934-1627

Aidan Kilcoyne
137 Berrian Road
Stamford, CT 06905

Robert McMahon
58 Berlin Street
Middleton, CT 06457

Matt Murphy
77 Fillow Street
Norwalk, CT 06855
(203) 866-7544

Robert O'Sullivan
121 Cottage Street
Trumbull, CT 06611
(203) 261-9041

William Shea
243 Spring Street
Torrington, CT 06790
(203) 482-6319

Ladies AOH State President
Marge Sheehan
75 Johnson Street
Trumbull, CT 06111
(203) 268-5109

Eire Philatelic Association
74 Woodside Circle
Fairfield, CT 06430
Contact: Michael Conway
(203) 367-9340

Friendly Sons of St. Patrick
37 Joseph Perkins Road
Norwich, CT 06360
Contact: William Cronin
(203) 886-1811

Gaelic-American Club
74 Beach Road
Fairfield, CT 06430
Contact: Charles Vaugh
(203) 254-2723
This full-fledged club, completed in 1993 has over 2,700 members and a variety of programs, including language classes, music lessons, step and set dancing and regular social activities.

Hartford Fire Department Emerald Society
4 Osage Road
West Hartford, CT 06117
Contact: Mike Gorman

Irish-American Community Center
9 Bennet Place
East Haven, CT 06512
(203) 469-3080
Hosts the annual Connecticut-Irish Festival each summer. Provides year 'round activities for the center's membership.

Irish-American Home Society
132 Commerce Street
Glastonbury, CT
(203) 633-9691

Pioneers of the Sacred Heart Total Abstinence Society
122 Grieb Road
Wallingford, CT 05492
Contact: Anna Mae McNulty
(203) 265-2446

West Haven Irish-American Club
92 Sumac Street
West Haven, CT 06516
Contact: Mary Carter

Willimantic Irish Club
PO Box 12
Willimantic, CT 06226
Contact: Betty Mohan

Pubs/ Restaurants

Irish Food Products

Curran Irish Imports
Ridgefield, CT
(203) 438-0776
Irish food products.

Pubs/ Restaurants

Bailey's Restaurant
262 Main Street
Route 25
Monroe, CT 06468
(203) 261-1399

Blackrock Castle
2895 Fairfield
Black Rock, CT 06605
Contact: Lena Smith
(203) 336-3990
Modeled after Blackrock Castle in Cork, Ireland. Fine dining and pub grub available, plus a Banquet Room. Live music on Thursdays, Fridays and Saturdays. Music session at 6:30 p.m. each Sunday led by Jim Sirch.

Brock's Pub
1209 Highridge Road
Stamford, CT 06905
Contact: Joe Loughran
(203) 357-1679
Irish food, music and entertainment throughout the year.

Jameson's Pub
600 Summer Street
Stamford, CT 06901
Contact: Pat Kennedy/Sean Tripodi
(203) 325-1131
Traditional Irish fare, with Guinness and harp on tap. Irish brunch served on Sunday's. Live traditional Irish music Thursdays and Saturdays.

J. F. O'Connell's Pub
360 Fairfield Avenue
Bridgeport, CT 06604
(203) 576-1004

South Street Saloon
109 South Street
Danbury, CT
(203) 748-9750

SERVICES

Services

Books

Celtic Book Merchants
27 Unquowa Road
Fairfield, CT 06430

Geneology

Lorrie Hamblin
342 Summit Street
Manchester, CT 06040
(203) 643-5398

Heritage Search
29 Thornton Drive
Newington, CT 06111
Contact: John Quinn
(203) 521-2619

Kevin McKenny
273 Oak Street
Manchester, CT 06040

Mormon Library
35-A Hynes Avenue
Groton, CT
(203) 449-8982

Mormon Library
Church of Jesus Christ of Latter Day Saints
Warpus Road
Madison, CT
(203) 245-8267

GIFT SHOPS

Fifth Province Irish Imports
64 Ridgeway Plaza
Stamford, CT 06905
Contact: Ann Murray
(203) 348-9603
Fairfield county's first ever Irish import shop has tapes, CD's, traditional music and many other gifts.

Irish Connections
660 Main Street South
Woodbury, CT 06798
Contact: Alice McLaughlin DeLuca
(203) 263-4748
Hats, handmade sweaters, gloves, scarves, Irish made and Irish oriented products available.

Irish Eyes
Olde Mystic Village
Mystic, CT 06355
Contact: Leda Lord
(203) 536-9960
A wide selection of Irish gifts are available.

Irish Sentiments
127 Washington Street
Norwalk, CT 06854
(203) 838-2287

The Life of Riley Irish Imports
890 Boston Post Road
Old Saybrook, CT 06475
Contact: Doraine Wall Riley
(203) 388-6002 Fax: (203) 399-6184
Great selection of Belleek, Drisden and Donegal china, Celtic jewelry, foods, tin whistles, CD's, cassettes, clothing, gifts, and Claddagh wedding bands.

Simon Pearce Glass
170 Main Street
Westport, CT 06880
(203) 226-2353
Mr. Pearce, a Cork native, carries on a family tradition of making Irish glassware using traditional techniques and materials. Catalogue available.

Twin Imports Irish Shop
346 Ethan Allen Highway
Ridgefield, CT 06877
(203) 431-6326

LEGAL SERVICES

Morrison & Swaine
Whitney Grove Square
2 Whitney Avenue, Suite 700
New Haven, CT 06510
Contact: Bruce Morrison
(203) 498-0086 Fax: (203) 782-9181
Law offices of former Connecticut Congressman whose legislation on immigration reform resulted in the Morrison Visa Program for Irish immigrants. Bruce Morrison is a foremost legal authority on immigration and Irish-American matters.

Publishers

Devin-Adair Co.
6 North Water Street
Greenwich, CT 06830
Contact: Roger Lourie
(203) 531-7755
Publisher of books and newsletters about Ireland. America's oldest publishing house of American-Irish topics was founded in 1911.

Greenwood Publishing Group
88 Post Road West
Westport, CT 06881
Contact: Kathleen Barrett
(203) 226-3571

Travel Agencies

European Travel Management, Inc.
237 Post Road West
Westport, CT 06880
(800) 922-7700
(203) 454-0090
Escorted tours, fly drive, golf holidays.

Gateway Travel
Box 503
Greenwich, CT 06830
(203) 531-7400
Tours to Ireland available.

Irish Links Tours and Travel
2701 Summer Street
Stamford, CT 06905
Contact: Maura Nolan
(203) 363-2088
(203) 363-2188 (fax)
Customized golf tours to Ireland, including fly-drive, escorted and tournament events.

Owenoak Castle Tours
3 Parklands Drive
Darien, CT 06820
(800) 426-4498
(203) 656-1651 (fax)
Official operators for Aer Lingus golf programs.

US Marketing
Box 3776
Danbury, CT 06813-3776
Contact: Tom Desantis
(203) 792-8677 1-800-452-9949
Serving the corporate and private sectors in sports, marketing, travel, PR, premium events tickets and promotional programs like the World Cup.

Wholesalers

Accent on Irish Wares, Ltd.
New Britain, CT
Contact: Heather Smith
(203) 827-8270

Curran Irish Imports
Ridgefield, CT
(203) 438-0776
Irish food products.

SERVICES

THE VOICE OF IRISH AMERICA

The Irish Voice Newspaper, Subscribe Today!

1 year (52 issues) only $25

Fill out the order form below,
(with Check or Money Order) and mail to:
IRISH VOICE NEWSPAPER
432 Park Avenue, South. Suite 1503
New York, New York USA 10016

Please send me a yearly subscription to the Irish Voice Newspaper:

Name: ______________________

Address: ______________________

____

Phone: ______________________

Signature: ______________ Date: ______________

Greenhorn Trading Company
Hartford, CT
Contact: Noreen Greene
(203) 524-8499

Guinness Import Co.
Guinness Place
6 Landmark Square
Stamford, CT 06901
(203) 323-3311
(203) 327-7642 (fax)
Distributors of Guinness, Harp and other Irish drinks.

Sports

New Haven Gaelic Football and Hurling Club
Contact: John Cullinan
(203) 772-7830

Stamford Gaelic Football Club
Contact: Don O'Dwyer
(203) 967-9774

Stamford Women's Soccer Club
Contact: Angela Donnelly

Hartford Gaelic Football Club
Contact: Michael Foley
(203) 563-4649

Maine's population: 1,227,928
Maine's Irish population: 217,265

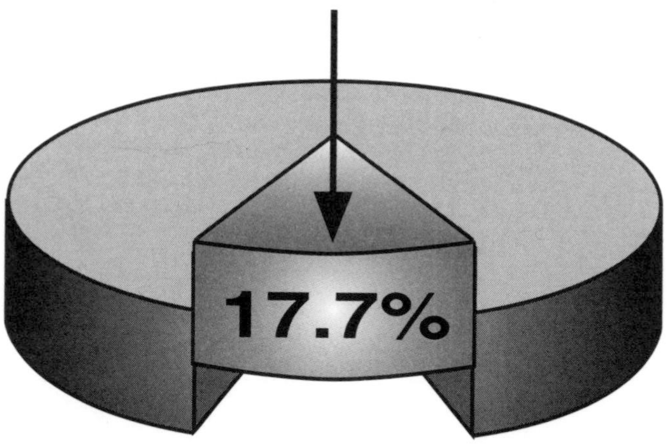

Annual Events

Parades

St. Patrick's Day Parade
West End Association
155 Brackett Street
Portland, ME
Contact: Eddie Murphy
(207) 774-9181
This annual parade is held on March 17th. It is a local parade for Portland's Irish-American community. The parade begins at the People's Building on Brackett Street and proceeds to the Harbor View Memorial Park where the Irish flag is flown over the city.

Other

St. Dennis Parish Annual Irish Picnic
Route 126
North Whitefield, ME
Contact: Fr. Eugene Gaffey
(207) 549-7425
Maine's oldest Irish event began over 100 years ago and features live Irish music, a chicken barbecue, an auction, a fresh produce sale, and plenty of activities for children.

Artisans

Celtic Art/Art

Val McGann Gallery
PO Box 395
Ogunquit, ME 03907
Contact: Anna McGann
(207) 967-4949
The Val McGann Gallery is located on Ocean Avenue, Kennebunkport, ME, where Irish landscapes, marine paintings, still life and florals are on display. For information on fund-raising exhibitions call 800-383-3167.

Education

Colleges & Universities

Bates College
Lewiston, ME 04240
(207) 786-6255 - English Dept.
Study abroad program at Trinity College, Dublin.

Colby College
Waterville, ME 04901
Contact: Patience-Ann Lank
(207) 872-3000
Undergraduate courses in Irish history; extensive collection of Irish literature. Junior year abroad at University College Cork.

New England College/ St. Francis College
Biddeford, ME 04005
(207) 283-0171 - English Dept.
Undergraduate courses in Yeats and Joyce.

St. Joseph's College
N. Windham, ME 04062
Contact: Mike Connolly
(207) 892-6766
A summer course for adult learners on the history of Ireland.

University of Maine
Orono, ME 04469
Contact: Nancy McKnight
(207) 581-3822 - English Dept.
Students can do an independent study in Irish literature. Periodic lectures on Irish, Scottish and Welsh literature.

University of Maine
Portland, ME 04103
Contact: Francis McGraff
(207) 780-4291
Undergraduate courses in Irish history and literature.

University of Southern Maine
Gorham, ME 04038
Contact: Mike Connolly
(207) 780-5215 - English Dept.
Undergraduate courses in Irish literature, history and Joyce.

Languages Classes

Ellsworth High School
Irish Language Classes
Box 405
Surry, ME 04684
Contact: Hugh Curran
(207) 667-7170
Adult education courses for beginners, spring and fall semesters.

Irish-American Club of Portland
PO Box 5205
Portland, ME 04101
Contact: Bartley Folan
(207) 799-6948
The Irish-American Club of Portland was founded in 1973 to promote Irish culture and tradition. The club sponsors Irish language, dance classes as well as concerts and trips.

Library Collections

Miller Library
Colby College
Mayflower Hill Drive
Waterville, ME 04901
(207) 872-3284
(207) 872-3555 (fax)
The Healy Collection of Irish literature contains several thousand volumes, chiefly Yeats, Joyce, Wilde, Shaw and other Irish literary Rennaissance writers, plus modern authors and support materials.

Portland Public Library
Congress Street
Portland, ME 04103
Contact: Arleen Carroll
(207) 871-1725
Several thousand volumes on Irish topics including the full set of Journals of the American-Irish Historical Society.

Music/Dance

Bands & Performers

Crooked Stovepipe Band
8 Sherbrooke Street
Portland, ME 04101
Contact: Mike Connolly
(207) 774-3392
The Crooked Stovepipe Band has been playing for dances, weddings, parties, and barn dances for almost 20 years and recently produced its first album.

Glenshane
PO Box 839
Rangeley, ME 04970
Contact: John Nesbitt/Jean McIntosh
(207) 864-2077
Accompanying themselves on guitar, bass, harmonica and penny whistle, John Nesbitt and Jean McIntosh, both hailing from Glenshane, combine rollicking and touching songs with humor and tall-tales.

Lazy Mercedes
PO Box 7664 DTS
Portland, ME 04112
Contact: George Worthley
(207) 828-8609
An original new folk duo with deep Celtic roots, they have performed concert tours from NY to Canada and have three albums to their credit.

Kevin McElroy
111 Bow Street
Freeport, ME 04032
(207) 865-3290
This traditional singer and instrumentalist performs Irish and other traditional music on a variety of instruments. He has over twenty years of experience in the US, Canada and Ireland. Recently released album, "Up the Winding River."

Northeast Winds
Box 860
Kennebunk, ME 04043
Contact: Allan McHale
Tel/Fax: (207) 967-3755
New England's Irish minstrels have been doing concerts for 15 years featuring Irish music and songs from the sea.

Portland Ceili Band
8 Sherbrooke Street
Portland, ME 04101
Contact: Mike Connolly
(207) 774-3392
The Portland Ceili Band performs for the regularly scheduled Irish-American Club Ceili's on the third Sunday of each month (except March, December and the summer months).

Sharon Pyne and Julia Lane
PO Box 168
Round Pond, ME 04564
(207) 529-5438
Lively, lilting dance tunes and haunting airs played on simple system traditional wooden flute by accomplished flutist Sharon Pyne and enhanced by the tasteful, spirited accompaniments of award wining Celtic harpist Julia Lane. Both have toured throughout the Northeastern USA and Ireland, playing at festivals, folk clubs, arts centers and ceili's. They have produced several recordings separately and recently released a duo album.

Reel Folk
16 Perkins Street
Topsham, ME 04086
Contact: Ralph Cheney
(207) 729-7949
Ralph Cheney, Nancy Stein, Doug Anderson, Carol Clark and George Worthley presents a varied program of music from Ireland and Scotland. This house band at Brian Boru's Pub in Portland mix it up from toe-tapping dance tunes to slow, graceful airs and are available for concerts and performances.

Tara's Minstrels
PO Box 7664 DTS
Portland, ME 04112
Contact: George Worthley
(207) 828-8609
Available for pubs, functions and weddings, Tara's Minstrels is an Irish trio with a distinct drive blended with New England sea songs.

Tom Wilsbach
PO Box 8489
Portland, ME 04101
(207) 773-7108
A traditional music performer on whistle and uilleann pipes. Music lessons available.

George Worthley
PO Box 7664 DTS
Portland, ME 04112
(207) 828-8609
Performs music from Scotland, Ireland and his native Maine. Available for clubs and functions throughout New England and will appear as a wandering kilted minstrel. George is considered one of the top Celtic bass players for studio work.

Kevin McElroy

Irish and American Music
Vocals, Guitar, Banjo

lll Bow Street
Freeport ME, 04032
(207) 865-3290

Dancing

Irish Set Dancers
8 Sherbrooke Street
Portland, ME 04101
Contact: Mike Connolly
(207) 774-3392
Irish set dancing practice is held on Tuesday nights at 7:00 p.m. in Portland (except in summer).

Dancing Teachers

Stillson School of Irish Dance
17 Highland Avenue
Gorham, ME 04038
Contact: Carlene Stillson, TCRG
(207) 839-2219
Classes for school aged children in traditional Irish step dancing and ceili. The children participate in competitions and demonstrations throughout New England and the east coast.

Instrument Sales

Jonathan Cooper
Violin Maker
RR2 Box 218
Sebago Lake, ME 04075
(207) 893-1866
A full service violin shop specializing in restoration, sales and new violin making. Appraisals and bow repairs also available.

Wood Sound Studio
Route 1
Glen Cove, ME 04846
Contact: Ron Pinkum
(207) 596-7407 1-800-696-7407
Wood Sound Studio makes violins, guitars and mandolins and repairs all types of stringed instruments. A full line of stringed instruments as well as flutes and tin whistles are available.

Radio Programs

The Harp and Bard
PO Box 2426
South Portland, ME 04106
Contact: Paul O'Neil
(207) 767-2291
WMPG 90.9 FM Portland, ME, is hosted by Paul O'Neil. The program features news and sports from Ireland as well as news of Irish organization and events in Maine. Traditional music and contemporary Irish ballads are just part of the mix.

New Potatoes
Radio Station WERU
Blue Hill Falls, ME 04615
Contact: George Fowler
(207) 374-2313
WERU 89.9 FM airs on Sundays from 4:00-6:00 p.m. A Celtic radio program featuring music from Ireland and the British Isles.

Television/ Cable

U.S.M. Community Cable TV
68 High Street
Portland, ME 04101
Contact: Caroline Hendry
(207) 780-5943
"Ireland Today" is a collection of videos on Irish topics such as community development education. Includes interviews with older first-second generation Portland Irish-Americans.

Organizations

Social Clubs

Ancient Order of Hibernians
The AOH was organized on May 4, 1836 in New York City. It played a pivotal role in helping Irish immigrants adjust to American society during the 19th century. Today the men's and women's branches of the AOH are active across the country promoting Irish culture, contributing to American values, Christian charity, the Catholic Church, supporting issues in Ireland and Northern Ireland and promoting, friendship and unity within the organization.

State President
Paul O'Neil
9 Trundy Road
Cape Elizabeth, ME 04107
(207) 767-2291

Askeaton, Limerick Project
74 Ferncroft Road
York, ME 03909
Contact: David Desmond
An effort to raise monies for the Askeaton Community Council, Limerick, to make the village a tourist attraction.

Irish-American Club of Portland
PO Box 5205
Portland, ME 04101
Contact: Bartley Folan
(207) 799-6948
The Irish-American Club of Portland was founded in 1973 to promote Irish culture and traditions. The club sponsors Irish language, dance classes, as well as concerts, dances and trips.

Maine Irish-American Club
135 Prentiss Street
Old Town, ME 04468
Contact: Jack Cashman
(207) 827-7460
The Maine Irish-American Club was established in 1992 to promote and preserve Irish culture, heritage and traditions, and to assist in the endeavors of Irish-Americans in the Bangor area.

The Maine Irish Children's Program
PO Box 3122
Portland, ME 04104
Contact: Susan and Bruce Schuyler
(207) 282-3939
A non-profit volunteer group sponsoring a six week summer program in Maine for 12 year old Catholic and Protestant children from Belfast. Founded in 1985, it promotes reconciliation in Northern Ireland by developing cross-community friendships in pre-teens through group activities in Belfast. Host family inquiries and donations welcome.

Pubs & Restaurants

Pubs

The Brian Boru
59 Center Street
Portland, ME 04101
Contact: Steve MacKenzie
(207) 780-1506
A traditional Irish pub featuring Irish music, food and ambience.

Keegan's Pub
Penobscott Inn
570 Main Street
Bangor, ME 04401
(207) 947-0566
1-800-468-2878
Keegan's offer a traditional pub with occasional live Irish entertainment. It's the meeting place for the Bangor Irish.

Services

BUSINESSES/ INVESTMENTS

Pan Atlantic Consultants
148 Middle Street
Portland, ME 04101
Contact: David Miley
(207) 774-6738
Dublin born David Miley will prepare feasibility, strategy and market research studies for companies locating to Ireland.

GENEALOGY

Eibhlin MacIntosh
P.O. Box 1144
York Harbor, ME 03911
Lecturer, teacher and researcher specializing in Irish-American family trees.

GIFT SHOPS

Celtic Designs Ltd.
414 Fore Street
Portland, ME 04101
Contact: Anita O'Donnell
(207) 773-8372
Celtic jewelery, capes, Book of Kells, scarves for women, tweed hats for men, brass, glass, vases and much more.

Ireland Crystal & Crafts
10 Exchange Street
Portland, ME 04101
Contact: Michael Furey
(207) 773-5832
A wide selection of competitively priced Irish goods including handmade arts and crafts, musical instruments, tapes, CD's, newspapers, books, magazines, with language classes and a social club.

Travel Agencies

All Points Travel
57 Route 35
Windham, ME 04062
Contact : Pat Mundy
(207) 892-8316 Fax: (207) 893-0537
With a great love for Ireland and much travel experience, independent and group tours can be organized.

Hemisphere Travel Service
5 Washington Street, Suite 27
Biddeford, ME 04005
1-800-848-4364
Books Irish folklore tours with Irish musician and folklorist Mick Moloney.

QuesTours International
PO Box 212 Lakeside Drive
Boothbay, ME 04537
Contact: Yvonne Kendley
(207) 633-7787 Fax: (207) 633-7787
QuesTours International specializes in European train travel for individual and group tours offering its guests a complimentary customized train excursion itinerary with time-table.

Other

Mary Alice Reilley Antiques
83 India Street
Portland, ME 04101
(207) 773-8815

Mary Alice Reilley Antiques
Two Lights Road
Cape Elizabeth, ME 04107
(207) 799-0638
Contact: Mary Alice Reilley
With two shops to choose from, Mary Alice Reilley Antiques specializes in Irish and English antiques. A wide variety of furniture, primitives and accessories are available and well stocked from regular purchasing visits to Great Britain.

Massachusett's population: 6,016,425
Massachusett's Irish population: 1,571,102

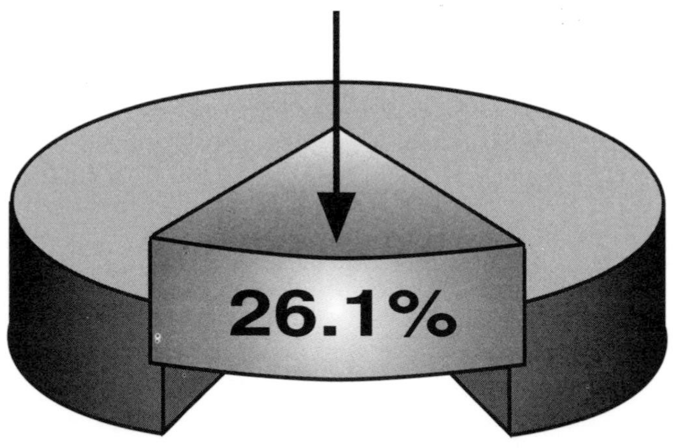

Annual Events

CONCERTS

Bank of Boston Celebrity Series
Symphony Hall
Massachusetts Avenue
Boston, MA 02118
(617) 482-2595
Presents the Chieftains each March at Symphony Hall, plus other Irish activities throughout the year.

Celtic Festival
Hatch Shell
The Esplanade
Boston, MA
Contact: Ed Pearlman
(617) 271-0958
Held each September at the Esplanade along the Charles River, this Celtic Festival showcases the finest Irish and Scottish musicians in greater Boston.

Comhaltas Tour of Champions
Waltham High School
Waltham, MA 02154
Contact: Larry Reynolds
(617) 899-0911
Each year in October Comhaltas Ceoltóirí Éireann sponsors a tour featuring some of the best musicians, singers, dancers and story tellers from all over Ireland.

FEISEANNA

For Feis information or to register a Feis, write to: Mrs. Patricia Dwyer, President, North American Feis Commission (NAFC), 17 Lillburn Drive, Stony Point, New York 10980.

April
Greater Boston Teachers Feis
Contact: Mary Heavey
(617) 325-0439

April
Greene-O'Leary-Madden Feis
Contact: Mary Madden
(617) 268-7086

May
Cohane School Feis
Contact: Maureen Cohane
(617) 327-9837

May
Committee of Greater Boston Teachers Feis
Contact: Joan Dunn
(617) 472-4813

May
Committee of Greater Boston Teachers Feis
Contact: Maura Nevin
(617) 749-7663

May
Massachusetts State Feis
Contact: Hiro Masuda
(508) 842-4836

June
Boston Feis
Contact: John Moran
(617) 862-8655
Senior Belt NAFC Championship.

June
Irish Heritage Feis
Contact: Rita O'Shea-Chaplin
(617) 665-3110

June
J. B. O'Reilly Feis
Contact: Catherine Maleckas
(413) 596-8222

November
Northeast Oireachtas
Andover, MA

December
Haley-Nevin School Feis
Contact: Maureen Haley
(617) 447-3081

December
O'Shea-Chaplin Feis
Contact: Rita O'Shea-Chaplin
(617) 665-3110

Festivals

February
Irish Focus Film Series
Boston College
Contact: Marie Jackson
(617) 552-8000
Featuring the best Irish films and documentaries by independent Irish filmmakers, held each winter.

June
Stonehill Irish Festival
Stonehill College
North Easton, MA 02357
Contact: Martin McGovern
(508) 281-1081
Sponsored by the Irish Cultural Center, this annual event feature the best Irish traditional and popular music available. Other activities include Gaelic football, equestrian demonstrations, lectures, and a market place featuring over 100 gift shops and craftspeople. Held the second weekend in June.

July
Billerica Irish Festival
Livingston Street
Tewksbury, MA
Contact: Deirdre Leger
(508) 667-3762
Held the third weekend in July, featuring the best Irish bands in New England.

July
Lowell Folk Festival
Lowell National Park Service
Contact: Sue Leggett
(508) 454-7060
Held the second weekend in July, featuring nationally acclaimed folk and Irish bands.

Parades

Boston St. Patrick's Day Parade
This annual parade through South Boston draws over a quarter of a million people.

Greater Lawrence St. Patrick's Day Parade
PO Box 275
Lawrence, MA 01842
Contact: Michael Coleman
(508) 686-4022
Started in 1983, the Parade is scheduled the Sunday following St. Patrick's Day. Join thousands of other parade viewers and see this grand tradition.

Holyoke St. Patrick's Day Parade
(401) 534-3376
The second largest Parade held in the US. Held the Sunday after March 17th.

Worcester County St. Patrick's Day Parade
Contact: Leo Quinn - (508) 753-7197
Contact: Judy Wilkinson - (508) 865-0229
This annual St. Patrick's Day Parade, held each March, features the color and pageantry of many groups, including the Shriners (an affiliation of the Burns Institute) and the Rose of Tralee Float, organized by Fr. John Cahill. The festivities begin the Friday before the parade with a banquet held in honor of the Grand Marshal, and the evening before the parade, they hold their Annual Mass.

OTHER

March
Irishman of the Year Award
Friends of Kennedy Library
Contact: Gerard Doherty
Held each year in March, the Award recognizes a preeminent Irish-American for embodying the spirit of John F. Kennedy. Past recipients have included William Bulger, Jim Brett and Ted Kennedy.

March
Irish Spring Shamrock Classic 5K Run
Dartmouth Street
Boston, MA
Contact: Sue Smith
(508) 655-6270
Held the first Sunday in March, this popular road race benefits Boston's Camp Joy program for disabled children. Prizes for men's, women's, seniors, wheelchair and children's races.

March
Irish Writers Series
Boston Parks Department
1010 Massachusetts Avenue
Boston, MA 02118
Contact: Michael Quinlin
(617) 635-4505 Fax: (617) 635-3104
Launched in March 1993, the Irish Writers Series highlights Ireland's literary achievements and supports Irish writing, arts and theater, both locally and from Ireland. Past participants in the series include Thomas Flanagan, Seamus Heaney, Morgan Llywelyn, John McGahern, and Nuala ní Dhomhnaill.

March
St. Patrick's Day Mass
Cathedral of The Holy Cross
1400 Washington Street
Boston, MA 02118
(617) 542-5682
Cardinal Bernard Law celebrates St. Patrick's Day mass at noon on March 17th at The Cathedral of The Holy Cross in the South End.

April
Irish Jewish Sedar
Temple Emanuel
385 Ward Street
Newton, MA
(617) 330-9696
Co-sponsored by the Archdiocese of Boston and the Anti-Defamation League, this annual April gathering celebrates Easter and Passover, and is part of an ongoing effort to strengthen ties between the Irish and Jewish communities of Boston.

April
Worcester Rose of Tralee
Contact: Mike O'Driscoll -
(508) 755-1036
Mike McCarthy - (508) 832-3746
Mike O'Driscoll, President of the Worcester Rose of Tralee, first started the Worcester chapter through his involvement with the Worcester Parade in 1982. They hold their annual Rose dance in April to choose the Worcester representative, the finalist competes in June with the other Massachusetts finalists and the overall winner then goes to Tralee in Ireland to represent Boston in August of each year.

May
The Michael Joyce Humanitarian Award
Friends of the Central Remedial Clinic
Boston Chapter
PO Box 201
Boston, MA 02133
Contact: Mary Joyce Morris
(617) 729-0621 Fax: (617) 756-0213
A fund-raising group to benefit the Michael Joyce Wing at the Clinic in Dublin, Ireland. The CRC serves all of Ireland and offers services to mentally and physically challenged children and adults. It is a leader in the treatment of its patients and also offers a support system for the family. They hold an annual dinner dance each May in honor of the award's recipients. Past honorees include Ambassador Flynn, Joseph Faherty, Rev. Bartley MacPhaidin, Noel Henry and Margaret Geraghty.

June
Boston Rose of Tralee Pageant
171 Waverly Street
Arlington, MA 02174
Contact: Eileen O'Sullivan
(617) 643-6694
This is an annual event to promote Irish culture and heritage. It is a pageant for girls of Irish descent aged from 19-25. They are judged on poise, personality, intelligence, graciousness and good dress sense. Contests start March through May with the grand final held in June. The lucky finalist wins a trip to Ireland for 10 days, representing Boston in Tralee, County Kerry.

June
James Joyce Ramble
Contact: Martin Hanley
(617) 329-9744
A 10K road race held the last sunday of April, complete with Joycean characters cheering from the sidelines. Starts in Dedham Square.

December
"Irish Christmas in Boston"
c/o Irish Immigration Center
Tremont Street
Boston, MA 02108
Contact: Lena Deevy/Patrick Riordan
(617) 367-1126
Sponsored each year by the Irish Immigration Center for those Irish not going home for the holidays. The Center also hosts a St. Stephen's Day brunch on December 26th.

Artisans

Celtic Art/Art

Curious Rabbit Gifts
331 East Street
Clinton, MA 01510
Contact: Cheryl Parabicoli
(508) 368-1610
Decorative paintings on welcome signs, slate and mailboxes, with an Irish theme. Irish phrases and Gaelic sayings, hand painted on plaques.

Seamus Healy
PO Box 247
West Dennis, MA 02670
(508) 394-0839
Handmade original water colors and poetry entitled, "Ireland O Ireland" which celebrates the West of Ireland.

Higgins & Ross Photography & Design
281 Princeton Street
North Chelmsford, MA 01863
(508) 454-4248 (tel/fax)

Kevin O'Brien
4 Wyatt Circle
Somerville, MA 02143
(617) 628-0161
Celtic illustrations and design, book jackets, posters and children's books.

David O'Docherty
252 Winthrop Street, #2
Winthrop, MA 02152
(617) 846-9504
Dublin born expressionist painter has held shows in Dublin, Paris, New York and Boston.

The Olde Celtic Shirtery
48 Cummings Avenue
Quincy, MA 02170
Contact: Sean O'Reilly
(617) 847-4238
Original adaptations of ancient Celtic art design on T-shirts, sweats, ties, documents, bodhráns, and custom applications upon request. Wide jewelry selections also available.

William O'Callaghan
257 West Tisbury Road
Edgartown, MA 02539
(508) 627-3151
Pottery maker with Celtic designs. Open year 'round.

Brian Queally
656 Adam Street
Dorchester, MA 02122
(617) 288-7670
Murals, portraits and landscapes.

Galleries

Aisling Gallery & Framing
229 Lincoln Street
Hingham, MA 02043
Contact: Maureen and John Connolly
(617) 749-0555 Fax: (617) 749-0177
The only art gallery in the US devoted exclusively to art of Ireland - oils, pastels, watercolors, limited editions, posters and prints from the National Gallery, Dublin. Classes in Irish literature, history, Gaelic language, poetry, violin, harp, bodhrán and tin whistle, Celtic calligraphy, painting, weekend trips to Irish theater in New York, local traditional music, concerts and plays.

Handmade Arts/Crafts

Chapel Hill Jewelers
80 North Street
Medfield, MA 02052
Contact: Joe Shea
(508) 359-5140
Celtic jewelry.

Joe Keane
96 Powderhouse Boulevard
Somerville, MA 02145
(617) 625-0243
Celtic jewelry.

Connie Kelly
Pat Maunsell
48 Bright Road
Belmont, MA 02178
(617) 484-8481
The Irish Thatched Cottage Exhibit, winners of the Award of Excellence and The Boston Globe People's Choice Award at the 1993 New England Spring Flower Show.

Storytelling

Joe Keane
96 Powderhouse Boulevard
Somerville, MA 02145
(617) 625-0243
Storyteller.

Sharon Kennedy
184 Palmer Street
Arlington, MA 02174
(617) 643-7101
Teller of Celtic fables and legends for children.

The New Vaudevillian
Contact: Peter O'Malley
(617) 536-6695
Named "Entertainer of the Year" by the Boston Parents' Paper, dubbed "ace Magician" by the Boston Herald, O'Malley is nationally and internationally acclaimed for his magic, puppets, story telling, organized games and contests, guitar and songs and audience participation.

Jay O'Callahan
Box 1054
Marshfield, MA 02050
(617) 837-0962
World renowned as a storyteller, O'Callahan was hailed by Time Magazine as "a genius among storytellers." He performed in Dublin's Abbey Theater in 1993, where he traded tales with numerous Irish storytellers. His books are published by Peachtree Publishers in Atlanta, GA. (404) 876-8761.

Maggi Peirce
544 Washington Street
Fairhaven, MA 02719
(508) 996-5295
Belfast native Maggi Peirce is an acclaimed storyteller, author, singer and teacher. Her program includes songs, ballads and recitations.

THEATER

New Ireland Arts
88 Fairfield Street
Needham, MA 02192
Contact: Joe Powers/Mike O'Connor
(617) 449-2796
New Ireland Arts is dedicated to presenting the very best Irish drama, story-telling, poetry and music.

The Poets' Theatre
61 Kirkland Street
Cambridge, MA 02138
Contact: Ann Warner
(617) 576-7638 Fax: (617) 495-0755
The Poets' Theater frequently produces works by Irish playwrights and poets, and sponsors Irish poetry readings.

Súgán Theater Company
32 Hawthorne Avenue
Arlington, MA 02174
Contact: Carmel O'Reilly
(617) 646-5983 Fax: (617) 466-2098
The Súgán Theater is dedicated to the production of plays that draws from the well of Celtic and Irish culture, with an emphasis on the contemporary. It seeks to support and foster Irish theatrical talent in the Boston area. Productions to date include "Away Alone," "The Lament for Arthur Cleary," "Mary and Lizzie," "Down the Flats" and "Mary Queen of Scotts Got Her Head Chopped Off." Call the above number to add your name to the mailing list and/or to inquire about upcoming events or to make reservations.

Writing

Sue Asci
(617) 436-1222
Editor and writer for the Irish Reporter.

Maureen Connolly
(508) 697-9322
Columnist for the Irish Echo.

Robert Connolly
(617) 426-3000
Covers Irish issues for The Boston Herald.

Kevin Cullen
(617) 929-2000
Covers Irish issues for The Boston Globe.

Irish Writers Series
Boston Parks Department
1010 Massachusetts Avenue
Boston, MA 02118
Contact: Michael Quinlin
(617) 635-4505 Fax: (617) 635-3104
Launched in 1993, the Irish Writers Series highlights Ireland's literary achievements and supports Irish writing, arts and theater, both locally and from Ireland.

Alan Loughnane
14 Centre Street
Cambridge, MA 02139
(617) 876-1568
Columnist for the Irish Voice.

Jay O'Callahan
Box 1054
Marshfield, MA 02050
(617) 837-0962
Author of many children stories about his childhood in Brookline, MA. His latest book, published by Peachtree Publishers in Atlanta, is entitled "Orange Cheeks." This world renowned storyteller was hailed by Time Magazine as "a genius among storytellers."

Maggi Peirce
544 Washington Street
Fairhaven, MA 02719
(508) 996-5295
Belfast native Maggi Peirce, an acclaimed author, storyteller, singer and teacher, is the author of "Keep the Kettle Boiling," "Storytellers Guide," and "Christmas Mince." She is presently writing a novel for young girls.

Daniel P. Murphy
19 Congress Street
Wilmington, MA 01887
Contact: Dan Murphy/Joan Murphy
(508) 657-5486
Dan Murphy is a nationally recognized poet. X. J. Kennedy has written, The Fractured Emerald "...contains so much feeling and takes in such a wide expanse of life; it's particularly welcome in these times of so much verse poetry that's cool and nugatory." Mr. Murphy is also a family therapist specializing in Irish families.

Education

Adult Community Courses

Cape Cod Community College
Route 132
West Barnstable, MA 02668
Contact: Bobbi Kelly
(508) 362-2131 ext. 455
Study tours to Ireland's Gaeltacht regions, including Kerry, Galway and the Aran Islands. Offers an advanced watercolors course in Ireland in the summer.

Dorchester Center for Adult Education (DCAE)
Dorchester, MA 02124
Contact: Mairin Keady
(617) 474-1170
Mairin Keady has a diploma in teaching Gaelic from University College Galway. She believes that Gaelic is an essential part of Irish heritage and encourages everyone to learn. She looks forward to lively discussions where language and Irish culture will be the focal points.

Irish Social Club of Boston
119 Park Street
West Roxbury, MA 02132
(617) 327-7306
Formed in 1945, the Irish Social Club has nearly 2,000 members. The club conducts weekly dances, plus music, language and dance lessons.

Colleges & Universities

Aquinas Junior College
15 Walnut Park
Newton, MA 02158
Contact: Sr. Fanchon Burke, CSJ
(617) 969-4400
Undergraduate courses on the history of Irish Literature.

Assumption College
400 Salisbury Street
Worcester, MA 01609
Contact: Michael O'Shea
(508) 752-5612 - English Dept.
Courses in Irish literature.

Bentley College
Waltham, MA 02254
Contact: Dennis Flynn
(617) 891-2000 - English Dept.
Courses in Irish literature.

Boston College (B.C.)
Irish Studies Program
Chestnut Hill, MA 02167
Contact: Kevin O'Neill/Adele Dalsimer
(617) 552-3938 Fax: (617) 552-3714
Thanks to a major commitment by the alumni of Boston College the Irish Studies Program has become perhaps the most extensive program in the US. Aside from the excellent courses available on both undergraduate and graduate levels, the Irish Studies Program also has an exchange program with University College Cork and Dublin's Abbey Theater. The Humanities Services brings in leading academics, artists, writers, and statespeople from Ireland. Boston College is co-publisher of the "Irish Literary Supplement," the leading American publication for Irish books and journals. The program has also developed an Irish music program, led by fiddle master Séamus Connolly, and an annual Irish film series.

Brandeis University
Waltham, MA 02254
(617) 736-2000 - English Dept.
Courses in Yeats, Beckett and Joyce.

Bridgewater State College
Bridgewater, MA 02324
Contact: Charles Fanning/
Maureen Connolly
(508) 697-1200 ext. 2283
English Dept.
Undergraduate and graduate courses in Irish literature and Irish immigration.

Clark University
950 Main Street
Worcester, MA 01610
Contact: Stanley Sultan
(508) 793-7431 - English Dept.
Contact: William Koelsch
(508) 793-7142 - History Dept.
Undergraduate and graduate courses on the Irish Literary Movement, Joyce, Yeats, O'Neill and F. Scott Fitzgerald.

College of the Holy Cross
Worcester, MA 01610
Contact: James Flynn
(508) 793-2443 - History Dept.
Courses for undergraduates in literature, politics and Irish history.

College of Our Lady of the Elms
Chicopee, MA 01013
Contact: Tom Moriarty
(413) 598-8351 - History Dept.
Undergraduate courses in Irish history and literature.

Emmanuel College
400 The Fenway
Boston, MA 02115
Contact: Mary Mason (617) 279-9340
Undergraduate courses in Anglo-Irish literature.

Fitchburg State College
Fitchburg, MA 01420
Contact: L. J. Arnold
(508) 345-2151 - History Dept.
Students can take a minor in Irish studies.

MASSACHUSETTS

VERITAS

Framingham State College
100 State Street
Framingham, MA 01701
Contact: Helen Heineman
(508) 620-1220
Undergraduate courses in Irish literature, Yeats and Joyce.

Gordon College
255 Grapevine Road
Wenham, MA 01984
Contact: Ann Ferguson
(617) 927-2300 - English Dept.
Undergraduate course on the Irish Renaissance.

Harvard University
Department of Celtic Languages and Literatures
61 Kirkland Street, 3rd Floor
Cambridge, MA 02138
Contact: Margo Granfors
(617) 495-1206 Fax: (617) 495-1010
Harvard offers day and evening undergraduate courses and programs on a variety of Irish topics. They also offer advanced (A.M. and Ph.D.) degrees. The Celtic Department hosts a symposium each spring that is published as a Proceedings. The Harvard Library has an excellent collection of over 20,000 books in Celtic Studies, plus a considerable number of original manuscripts and photostated facsimiles. The Center for Literary and Cultural Studies hosts a Celtic Seminar Series that offers a variety of programs open to the public throughout the year. The Friends of Harvard Celtic Studies can be reached at (617) 496-6305.

Massasoit Community College
Brockton, MA 02402
Contact: James Cottom
(508) 588-9100
Undergraduate courses in Irish history from the 1800's to the present day.

Merrimack College
Turnpike Road
North Andover, MA 01845
Contact: Catherine Murphy
(617) 683-7111 - English Dept.
Undergraduate courses in modern Irish literature.

North Adams State College
North Adams, MA 01247
Contact: J. P. Sullivan - English Dept.
(413) 664-4511
Undergraduate courses in Irish art and architecture.

Northeastern University
360 Huntington Ave.
Boston, MA 02215
Contact: Beth Cameron
(617) 437-4443
Irish courses in literature and history.

Regis College
235 Wellesley Street
Weston, MA 02193
Contact: Mary Malany
(617) 893-1820 - English Dept.
Offers undergraduate courses on Irish writers, a seminar on Yeats and Joyce, and a junior Year Abroad Program to Ireland.

Simmons College
Boston, MA 02115
Contact: David Sullette
(617) 738-2143 - English Dept.
Undergraduate courses in Anglo-Irish literature.

Southeastern Massachusetts University
Old Westport Road
North Dartmouth, MA 02747
Contact: Vernon Inghram
(617) 999-8605 - English Dept.
Undergraduate course on the Irish Literary Revival.

Stonehill College
Irish Studies Program
North Easton, MA 02357
Contact: Richard Finnegan
(508) 230-1135 Fax: (508) 230-1417
In addition to the extensive Irish courses available at the College, Stonehill also offers students a semester in Irish studies at University College Dublin and internships in Dublin. It presents a community lecture series, musical and cultural events, poetry readings, and lectures by politicians and scholars. The recently acquired "Archive of Irish Government Official Publications 1992-1993" offers a unique collection of government documents for research.

EDUCATION

Tufts University
Medford, MA 02155
Contact: Bernard McCabe
(617) 381-3170 - English Dept.
Graduate and undergraduate courses in Irish literature.

University of Lowell
One University Avenue
Lowell, MA 10854
Contact: Joseph Lipchitz
(617) 452-5000 - English Dept.
Graduate courses in Irish literature and problems of modern Ireland.

University of Massachusetts/ Amherst
Irish Studies Program
Amherst, MA 01003
Contact: Peggy O'Brien
(413) 545-5509
The Irish Studies program includes courses from U. Mass., Amherst College, Hampshire College, Mt. Holyoke College, and Smith College. It offers a wide range of courses in Irish literature, history, art, folklore, language and Irish-American history. It has an exchange program with University College Cork, and two programs in Dublin. U. Mass/ Amherst also has an extensive Irish library collection, including the Alspach Yeats Collection, a major resource for students interested in Irish literature.

University of Massachusetts/ Boston Irish Studies Program
Harbor Campus
Boston, MA 02125
Contact: Thomas O'Grady
(617) 929-8363
The Irish Studies Program is an interdisciplinary program designed to provide students with an opportunity to study Irish and Irish-American culture, primarily through literature and history. Course offerings cover major aspects of Irish culture from ancient times to present. Six courses are required for completion of the Irish Studies Program. Courses include a History of Boston, the Immigration in American Society: 1880-1924, and The Kennedys of Boston.

Wellesley College
Wellesley, MA 02181
Contact: Evelyn Barry
(617) 235-0320 - Music Dept.
Offers advanced study courses on Irish writers.

Westfield State College
Western Avenue
Westfield, MA 01086
Contact: Catherine Shannon
(413) 568-3311 - History Dept.
Undergraduate and graduate courses in Irish literature, drama, history and modern Ireland. Evening courses also available.

Wheaton College
Norton, MA 02766
Contact: Kathleen Vogt
(617) 285-7722
Courses in modern Irish literature with Study Abroad Programs in Cork and Dublin.

Wheelock College
Boston, MA 02115
Contact: Christina Moustakis
(617) 734-5200 - English Dept.
Undergraduate courses in modern Irish history.

Williams College
Williamstown, MA 02137
Contact: Don Gifford
(413) 597-2211 - English Dept.
Undergraduate course on James Joyce.

Worcester State College
Worcester, MA 01601
(508) 793-8000 - English Dept.
Studies on Yeats, Irish literature and the history of Ireland.

Conferences

Boston's Jews and Irish Conflict and Communality Conference
Boston College
Chestnut Hill, MA 02167
Contact: Professor John Michalczyk
(617) 552-4295 - Fine Arts Dept.
Co-sponsored by the Boston College Irish Studies Program and the Anti-Defamation League. This annual April conference addresses historical issues that parallel the Irish and Jewish races.

Language Classes

Aisling Gallery & Framing
229 Lincoln Street
Hingham, MA 02043
Contact: Maureen and John Connolly
(617) 749-0555 Fax: (617) 749-0177
Classes in Irish literature, history, Gaelic language, poetry, violin, harp, bodhrán and tin whistle, Celtic calligraphy, painting, weekend trips to Irish theater in New York, local traditional music concerts and plays.

Ár dTeanga Féin
The Gaelic Language Organization of Worcester
c/o The Irish Club
564 Millbury Street
Worcester, MA 01610
Contact: Kenneth Peterson
(508) 797-9482
The Gaelic Language Organization of Worcester has held free Irish language classes throughout central New England since 1986. Classes begin each September and January; class locations vary outside Worcester. For additional information send a S.A.S.E to Irish Language Study, PO Box 2465, Acton, MA 01720.

Boston College (B.C.)
Chestnut Hill, MA 02167
Contact: Phil O'Leary
(617) 552-8000
As part of it's extensive Irish Studies program, B.C. offers accredited language courses.

Cape Cod Community College
Route 132
West Barnstable, MA 02668
(617) 362-2131 ext. 455
Study tours to Ireland's Gaeltacht regions, including Kerry, Galway and the Aran Islands.

Peggy Cloherty
35 Vernon Street
Brookline, MA 02146
Organizes many of the Cumann na Gael's activities in the greater Boston area.

Cumann na Gaeilge i mBoston
Box 164
Dedham, MA 02026
Contact: Mary Concannon:
(617) 769-0059
John McGrath: (617) 326-3944
Jim West: (508) 369-4979
Dedicated to the preservation and promotion of the Irish language, this group sponsors language classes, functions and an annual Feis, held at Stonehill College each May. Monthly meetings are held every fourth Sunday at Emmanuel College. Membership includes a monthly newsletter and access to a lending library. Currently, courses for beginner, intermediate and conversation Irish are conducted in Dedham, Belmont, Dorchester and Brookline.

Harvard University
Celtic Studies Dept.
61 Kirkland Street, 3rd Floor
Cambridge, MA 02138
Contact: Margo Granfors
(617) 495-1206
The Celtic Department has a world renowned reputation for Celtic studies. *See fuller description in the Colleges/ Universities section.*

Willie Mahon
(617) 628-6173
Irish for beginners, advanced students.

Library Collections

Ancient Order of Hibernians
Division 8
9 Appleton Street
Lawrence, MA 01840
Contact: Dave Burke
(508) 687-8937
The AOH Club's Library in Lawrence has an excellent collection of nearly 2,000 books, newspapers, pamphlets, and other information on Ireland.

Alspach Yeats Collection
U/Mass Jones Library
Amherst, MA 01003
(413) 256-4090
A major resource for students of Irish literature.

Archdiocese of Boston Archives
2121 Commonwealth Avenue
Brighton, MA 02135
(617) 254-0100
The Archdiocese has a wealth of information on Irish immigration to Boston, especially in regard to the charitable institutions under the auspices of the Catholic Church, including correspondences of Cardinal O'Connell.

Boston Public Library (BPL)
Copley Square, Boylston Street
Boston, MA 02199
Contact: Liam Kelly
(617) 536-5400
The Irish material in the BPL is outstanding in scope and depth as the library continues to add to its strong base from the 19th century. In addition to the extensive reference holdings, there are many books for circulation, including books in Irish.

Burns Library
Boston College
Chestnut Hill, MA 02167
Contact: Bob O'Neill
(617) 552-3282
The Burns Library at Boston College houses the University's special Irish collection. This collection includes rare books, manuscripts, special editions, and original research materials. It recently acquired the largest Yeats collection in the world. The Burns Library also houses the B.C. Irish Music Archives, which contain over 500 rare recordings of Irish traditional music.

Mary Joan Glynn Library of Anglo Irish Literature
Stonehill College
North Easton, MA 02357
Contact: Madeline Foster
(508) 230-1395
This Library has over 1,500 titles, mostly on Irish Literature and poetry, but also on contemporary Irish issues, and a stately reading room where current Irish-American papers are available. It recently acquired the full collection of Irish government documents from 1922 to present date.

John F. Kennedy Library and Museum
Columbia Point
Boston, MA 02125
Contact: Frank Rigg
(617) 929-4557
The nation's memorial to President John Fitzgerald Kennedy. The museum portrays the life of our only President of Irish Catholic heritage, beginning with the arrival in Boston in 1848 of his great grandfather Patrick Kennedy of Wexford.

New England History Genealogical Society Library
101 Newbury Street
Boston, MA 02116
(617) 536-5740
NEHGS is the publisher of "The Search for Missing Friends", Irish immigrant advertisements placed in the Boston Pilot. They also sell books on Irish Genealogy. Please write for free catalog and brochure.

Plymouth Public Library
Irish Collection
132 South Street
Plymouth, MA 02360
Contact: Lee Regan
(508) 830-4250 Fax: (508) 830-4258
The Irish Collection was started by the generous donation of a library trustee and continues to be supported by the local chapter of the Ancient Order of Hibernians. Programming enhances the collection such as discussion groups on Lady Gregory, William Butler Yeats, John Millington Synge and Seán O'Casey. Other programs are planned.

Thomas P. O'Neill Library
Boston College
Chestnut Hill, MA 02167
Contact: Jeremy Slinn
(617) 552-4470
The O'Neill Library has an extensive collection of books and journals relating to Ireland. Subject areas emphasized are Irish history, government, poetry, drama, literature, and genealogy. The library has an extensive collection of Irish newspapers on microfilm, including such titles as The Irish Times, The Cork Examiner, The Freeman's Journal and The Irish Independent.

Widner Library
Harvard University
Cambridge, MA 02138
(617) 495-2411
The Harvard Library has an excellent collection of over 20,000 books on Celtic studies, plus a considerable number of original manuscripts and photostated facsimiles.

Other

Great Hunger Memorial Project
JFK PO Box 6366
Boston, MA 02114
Contact: Bill O'Donnell
(617) 722-4300
In May 1993, members of the Great Hunger Memorial Project and leaders of the Irish community in Boston and New England dedicated a temporary granite marker in memory of the victims of Ireland's Great Hunger. That engraved stone, located in Faneuil Hall Marketplace near the Boston Port's original water line, will be the site of a permanent Great Hunger Memorial funded and built by the grandchildren of the immigrants of the nineteenth century. The design for the memorial statue will be selected in 1994 and a publicly subscribed fundraising campaign is underway to underwrite the costs of what will be America's first permanent memorial to the victims of the Great Hunger of 1840-1847. Contributions can be mailed to the above address.

Music/Dance

Bands & Performers

The Alehouse Ceili Band
Contact: Tony Heggarty
(617) 329-6034
House band for the Old Irish Alehouse in Dedham.

The Bards
Contact: Jimmy McArdle
(413) 782-3909

Peter Barnes
(617) 259-8442
Piano.

The Boston Irish
118 Avon Street
Malden, MA 01248
Contact: Mossie Coughlan
(617) 324-8548
Music, including traditional Irish music for all occasions.

Boston Police Gaelic Column of Pipes & Drums
372 Cornell Street
Boston, MA 02131
Contact: Jim Barry
(617) 327-7875
This 45-member pipes and drums band specializing in Irish pipe music participates in concerts, festivals and parades. Music lessons are also available.

The Boys of Wexford
Contact: David Bagnell
(508) 761-9245

Brehon's Law
132 Portland Street
Boston, MA 02114
Contact: Ned Giblin
(617) 367-8370
House band for Paddy Burke's Pub in Boston.

Bridget & The Clovers
Contact: Bridget Gilmartin
(617) 356-4508

IRISH & AMERICAN MUSIC FOR ANY OCCASION

Black Velvet Band

508-657-8521
617-246-0481

MAKE YOUR FUNCTION THE ONE THEY'LL REMEMBER

Seamus Connolly
Irish Traditional Fiddler

Recordings
Notes from My Mind
Here and There
Banks of the Shannon
Warming Up

For Booking Information
(508) 970-0419
P.O.Box 547
Lowell, MA 01853

Brendan Bulger
492 East Broadway
Suite 310
South Boston, MA 02127
(617) 268-4414
All Ireland fiddler from South Boston with a new album entitled "The Southern Shore."

Chris Bulger
(617) 268-4414
Accordion playing in the Billy Caples tradition.

Casterbridge Union
Contact: Dan O'Neill
(508) 771-6328

Castlebay Duo
230 Lowell Street
Waltham, MA 02154
Contact: Watch City Arts, Bob Weiser
(617) 647-1075
The Castlebay Duo is comprised of Julia Lane, an award-wining Celtic harpist and vocalist; and Fred Gosbee, a 12-string guitarist, 5-string viola and woodwind musician, a baritone and writer. They play at festivals, folk clubs and arts centers from Maine to Maryland and they have four recordings on the Outer Green label.

Aoife Clancy
(508) 559-9216
Singer.

Connaught Ceili Band
Contact: Tommy Sheridan
(617) 923-1627

Jimmy Connelley
(617) 471-4545
Sean Nos singer.

Mike Connolly and Celtic Aires
(617) 924-0242

Seamus Connolly
Lowell, MA
(508) 970-0419
A Clare native and ten-time All-Ireland fiddle champion, Connolly is an accomplished master musician who has helped to enhance and elevate Irish music throughout New England and across the US. He has several albums available on The Green Linnet label and teaches Irish music at Boston College. Also available for private lessons.

Tony Cuffe
Arlington, MA
Vocals, harp and guitar
(617) 643-8559
Scottish guitar, harp, mandelin and vocals. Performs solo and with other musicians. Available for lessons.

Johnny Cunningham
(617) 965-5494
Fiddle.

Curragh's Fancy
Contact: Bobby Foulkes
(617) 296-2113

Dennis Curtin Band
Contact: Jerry Baily
(617) 391-5716

Joe Derrane
(617) 963-6239
Accordion.

Mairéad Doherty
(508) 653-7480
Harpist, vocalist and recitations. Available for weddings, functions and concerts.

Dooley Brothers
(617) 268-0734

Pat Dunlea
(617) 581-3797
Singer and banjo player.

Emerald Stars
105 Willow Street
West Roxbury, MA 02132
Contact: Frank Kerwick
(617) 469-2668
Music for weddings, parties, socials and dances.

Erin's Melody
Contact: Margaret Dalton
(617) 696-1702

Sheila Falls
(508) 699-5518
Fiddle.

Pete Farley
(413) 586-0712
Banjo.

John Farrell
(617) 471-8332
Drums, guitar and vocals. Recording studio.

The Ferry Men
Contact: Pat King - (617) 927-0869
Dermot O'Keefe - (617) 942-1176

Bridie Fitzgerald
(617) 444-0115
Singer.

Sean and Colum Gannon
Dorchester, MA
(617) 436-9598
Accordion.

Jim Gleason
(617) 429-7529
Flute.

Joe Glynn and the Irish Mist
(617) 769-5989

Kathleen Guilday
22 Norfolk Place
Sharon, MA 02067
(617) 784-8750
All Ireland champion harpist, Guilday performs throughout New England.

Andy Hanley
Boston
(617) 282-9652
Fiddle.

The Healeys
Contact: Donnie Healey/Sheila Healey
(413) 592-2842

Andy Healy Band
(617) 965-2193
Weddings, banquets, concerts, pubs, Irish music for all occasions.

Noel Henry's Irish Showband
PO Box 91
Kingston, MA 02364
Contact: Valerie
(617) 934-2200
(617) 934-5708 (fax)
Professional Irish-American dance band for concerts, dances, weddings and anniversaries. Ten recordings on tapes, albums and CD's.

Jim Hogan
(617) 696-1569
Flute.

Gary and Linda Hudson
(508) 794-8325
Celtic percussion and fiddles.

In memory of

Micho Russell

from Doolin County Clare • 1915-1994
Rest in Peace
Sadly missed by his friends of
County Clare in Boston

Joe Joyce
(617) 269-2276
Accordion.

The Jug O'Punch
(508) 365-5980

Kathy and the Irish-Americans
Contact: Kathy Moloney
(617) 769-9165

The Keane Family
Contact: Fergus Keane
(508) 668-6983
Accordion, flute, guitar and vocals.

Paddy Keenan
(508) 653-5351
Uilleann pipes.

Billy Kelly
(617) 859-8094
Banjo, guitar and vocals.

The Kelly Family
Contact: Sally Kelly/Jimmy Kelly
(617) 244-3985
Piano, banjo, fiddle and pipes.

Maureen Kelly-Reynolds
(508) 653-5351
Piano accordion.

Tommy Kelly
(617) 332-0589
Scottish pipes.

Keltic Kids
19 Congress Street
Wilmington, MA 01887
Contact: Daniel Murphy/Joan Murphy
(508) 657-5486
The "Keltic Kids" are nationally recognized traditional Irish musicians. Gráinne, a fiddler, is a 3-time North American Champion and placed 3rd in the 1992 World Championship. Daniel is a 3-time North American Champion on bodhrán and Patrick is champion on whistle.and is also a step dancer. They are available for traditional Irish music and dance for all occasions.

Kerry Blues Band
Contact: Gerry Lynch
(617) 665-3820

Kick The Can
Contact: Paul Kenny
(617) 698-7059

Helen Kissell
(617) 926-8302
Piano, flute and whistle.

Julia Lane
230 Lowell Street
Waltham, MA 02154-5072
Contact: Watch City Arts, Bob Weiser
(617) 647-1075
This Celtic harpist and vocalist has been described as energetic and innovative. Her recording entitled "Harvest" is available on the Outer Green label.

Alan Loughnane
14 Centre Street
Cambridge, MA 02139
(617) 876-1568
Fiddle, mandolin, vocals, performing, recording and promotions.

Willie Mahon
(617) 628-6173
Vocalist, whistle and flute.

Tommy Mallet
(617) 436-9598
Flute.

Brian Malone
(617) 497-9196
Singer.

Laurel Martin
(508) 692-6802
Fiddler.

Pat McDonagh
(508) 755-1659
Irish DJ, central Massachusetts.

Mike McDonough
(508) 388-3485
Accordion.

Martin McEntee
(617) 479-6750

Kevin McGowan
230 Lantern Road, #17
Revere, MA
(617) 286-8814
Singer.

Dickie McManus and the Irish Revolution
(617) 284-3175
Weddings and concerts.

Jim McNally
155 Church Street
Clinton, MA 01510
Contact: James McNally
(508) 365-5980
Chef and owner of The Old Timer Restaurant, Jim McNally, an Irish tenor, performs Wednesdays and weekends.

Áine Minogue
97 Bow Street, #2
Arlington, MA 02146
(617) 641-0903
Tipperary native, singer, composer and Celtic harpist. Áine Minogue has two albums to her credit, the most recent entitled, "Were you at the Rock" which is available on cassette and CD. Available for concerts, banquets, festivals, weddings, workshops and private tutoring.

Joe Moriarty & The Irish Beat
(617) 266-1504

Danny Moylan
(617) 825-4373
Drums.

Brian Myers
97 Bow Street, #2
Arlington, MA 02146
(617) 641-2146
Mandelin, guitar and bazouki.

Russ Myers
97 Bow Street, #1
Arlington, MA 02146
Vocalist.

Jimmy Noonan
(617) 738-5230
Flute player with recently released album entitled "The Clare Connection."

Kevin O'Brien
4 Wyatt Circle
Somerville, MA 02143
(617) 628-0161
Fiddle and uilleann pipes.

Pat and Kay O'Brien
(617) 391-7540
Accordion and vocals.

Tom O'Carroll
(508) 462-9954
Singer.

Robbie O'Connell
(617) 528-4151
Singer/songwriter.

David O'Docherty
(617) 846-9504
Flute.

Billy O'Neill
Accordion.

Tony O'Riordan
(508) 528-4151
Singer.

Alfie O'Shea
(508) 559-9472
Singer.

Maggi Peirce
544 Washington Street
Fairhaven, MA 02719
(508) 996-5295
Belfast native Maggi Peirce is an acclaimed singer, author, storyteller and teacher. Her program includes songs and ballads, recitations and storytelling.

Larry Reynolds
(617) 899-0911
Fiddler and Comhaltas president, Reynolds, a Galway native, is one of the most high profile Irish musicians in New England. Reynolds leads a number of sessions around the greater Boston area including The Green Briar session on Monday evenings.

Larry Reynolds, Jr.
(617) 326-8616
Accordion.

Mike Reynolds
(617) 698-2256
Accordion, guitar and vocals.
This versatile musician recently released a new album entitled "Tara Hill."

Phyllis Reynolds
(617) 899-0911
Piano.

Seán Reynolds
(617) 899-0911
Fiddle.

Heather Ross Feldmath
(617) 493-7190
Celtic harpist.

Barbara Russell
(413) 259-1742
Harpist.

John Shea
(617) 470-2351
Fiddle.

Tommy Sheridan
(617) 489-2224
Accordion.

Mike Soles
44 Anchorage Court
Harwichport, MA
(508) 430-2026
Guitar and vocals.

Silver Spears
Contact: Tim Leary
(617) 337-4983

Spinner's Lilt
c/o 205 Worcester Court
Falmouth, MA 02540
Contact: Bill Black
(508) 540-6899 Fax: (508) 540-4356
Some say they are "the greatest ceili band on Cape Cod."

Fintan Stanley
(617) 786-9742
Piano accordion.

Sunday's Well
Contact: Ned
(508) 385-7606

Beth Sweeney
(617) 552-8495
Fiddle.

Liam Tiernan
(617) 464-0460
Guitar and vocalist with several albums including "Liam Tiernan" and "One for the Ditch."

Brendan Tonra
(617) 923-0062
Fiddle.

Tradition
Contact: Aidan Maher
(617) 479-1178

Fergus Tuohig
(617) 789-5619
Banjo.

John Van Kirk
(617) 524-9054
Stringed instruments.

Shay Walker
(617) 523-0291
Guitar and vocals.

Johnny Walsh
(617) 825-1538
Accordion.

Patsy Whelan
(508) 465-2785
Singer.

The Wild Rover
84 Union Street
Norfolk, MA 02056
Contact: Alan Deeb
(508) 528-2488
Performing since 1986, Steve O'Callaghan, Alan Deeb, Carmine DiMascio and Kevin Cronin make up this Boston-based band. They are popular at clubs, pubs, cruises, weddings, anniversaries and birthday's for their wide variety of music, from Popular, Country, Rock and Roll to ethnic (specialty being Irish).

Dancing Adjudicators

Josephine Fitzmaurice Moran
12 Fairbanks Road
Lexington, MA 02173
(617) 862-8655

Maureen Greene O'Leary
1568 High Street
Westwood, MA 02090
(617) 551-0945

Colleen Marie Griffith
85 East India Row-8C
Boston, MA 06357
(617) 367-0262

Noreen Houlihan Smith
2066 Dorchester Avenue
Boston, MA 02124
(617) 265-3308

Edward Irwin
30 Alroy Road
South Weymouth, MA 02190
(617) 337-7648

Noreen Melvin
96 Walnut Street
Brookline, MA 02146
(617) 566-1852

Rita O'Shea
5 Youle Street
Melrose, MA 02176
(617) 665-3110

Michael Smith
2066 Dorchester Avenue
Boston, MA 02124
(617) 265-3308 (617) 471-1894

Dancing Ceili/Set

Con and Phil Murphy
Springfield, MA
(413) 788-8603

Comhaltas Set Dancers
Contact: Sally Harney
(508) 688-3473

Dancing Teachers

Frances Campbell Connolly
113 Spruce Street
Watertown, MA 02172
(617) 926-8170 (617) 789-4222

Lisa Chaplin
311 Upham Street
Melrose, MA 02176
(617) 662-2191 (617) 956-5002

Maura Clifford Nevin
4 Stone Gate Lane
Hingham, MA 02043
(617) 749-7663

Sheila Cloherty Laskey
78 Hooker Avenue, #17
Somerville, MA 02144
(617) 776-3832

Mary Jo Connell
103 Parsons Street
Brighton, MA 02135
(617) 787-2726

Kathleen Costello
54 Temi Road
Brockton, MA 02402
(508) 583-3719

Mary Costello Madden
1596 Columbia Road
South Boston, MA 02127
(617) 268-7086

John Cunniffe
475 Shawmut Avenue
Boston, MA 02116
(617) 247-6993

Christine Duffin
40 Blanchard Road
South Weymouth, MA 02190
(617) 337-5473

Josephine Fitzmaurice Moran
12 Fairbanks Road
Lexington, MA 02173
(617) 862-8655

Mary Forbes
37 Edgemere Road
Quincy, MA 02169
(617) 479-4860

Joan Forbes Dunn
38 Woodward Avenue
Quincy, MA 02169
(617) 472-4813

Maureen Greene
71 Belle Avenue
West Roxbury, MA 02132
(617) 323-0872

Maureen Greene O'Leary
1568 High Street
Westwood, MA 02090
(617) 551-0945

Colleen Marie Griffith
85 East India Row-8C
Boston, MA 06357
(617) 367-0262

Brenda Hamilton
24 Elijah Street
Woburn, MA 01801
(617) 935-0265

Maureen Anne Hamilton
180 Central Street, #12
Stoneham, MA 02180
(617) 438-6278

Maureen Hansen Keohane
217 Weld Street
West Roxbury, MA 02131
(617) 327-9837

Harney Academy of Irish Dance
538 Elm Road
Walpole, MA 02081
Contact: Liam Harney
(508) 668-3473
Classes taught by world champion step dancer Liam Harney. Instruction in ceili, set and step dancing styles. Classes for children and adults.

Mary Heavey
31 Whitford Street
Roslindale, MA 02131
(617) 325-0439

Ann Marie Hennessey
366 Quincy Avenue, #604
Quincy, MA 02169
(617) 471-4396

Noreen Houlihan Smith
2066 Dorchester Avenue
Dorchester, MA 02124
(617) 265-3308

Maureen King Haley
47 Belcher Drive
Whitman, MA 02382
(617) 447-3081

Bridget Lynch
35 Newbury Avenue
North Quincy, MA 02171
(617) 328-6525

Mary Lynch
78 Sheldon Street
East Milton, MA 02186
(617) 773-9416

Sheila MacPherson
29 Kerry Lane
East Taunton, MA 02718
(508) 822-9979

Maureen McDermott Ziskowski
34 Northridge Road
Westfield, MA 01085
(413) 562-2896

Elizabeth McGuire
83 Barbour Terrace
Quincy, MA 02169
(617) 471-3479

Mary McInerney
8 Clara Street
Worcester, MA 01606
(508) 852-5544 (508) 853-9192

Sheila Milmore Bremer
17 Bellis Circle
Cambridge, MA 02140
(617) 497-1038

Rita O'Shea
5 Youle Street
Melrose, MA 02176
(617) 665-3110

Michael Smith
2066 Dorchester Avenue
Boston, MA 02124
(617) 265-3308 (617) 471-1894

Deirdre Sullivan
41-6 Angleside Road
Waltham, MA 02154
(617) 891-3286

Clare Sullivan Freeman
100 Commandants Way, #201
Chelsea, MA 02150
(617) 884-6282

Instrument Repairs

Chris Abel
(617) 369-7114
Flutemaking and repairs.

The Button Box
9E Pleasant Street
Amherst, MA 01002
Contact: Doug Creighton
(413) 549-0171 Fax: (413) 253-7475
The Button Box specializes in the sale and repair of accordions and concertinas. Besides their ever-changing stock of new and used Irish-style instruments, they carry instructional books and tapes, Irish song and tune books and a large selection of traditional and modern Irish music in CD and cassette formats. Call or write for a free catalog.

Instrument Sales

The Music Emporium
2018 Massachusetts Avenue
Cambridge, MA 02140
Contact: Michael Mele
(617) 661-6977
The Music Emporium carries a large selection of Irish instruments, including banjo, bouzouki, guitar, pennywhistle, concertinas and bodhráns, as well as books and tapes. Music lessons are also available.

Sandy's Music Shop
896 Massachusetts Avenue
Cambridge, MA 02138
Contact: Sandy Sheehan
(617) 491-2812
Specializing in fiddles, banjos and mandlins both for sale and repair. Wide selection of music books, accessories and tapes.

Walton Music
Box 1505
Westfield, MA 01085
Contact: Leo Doherty
1-800-541-5004
Sixty years as an instrument maker of bodhráns, tin whistles, harps, musical videos, musical instructions and songbooks.

Comhaltas Ceoltoiri Eireann

Hanafin-Cooley Branch of Boston

• Session
the first Sunday of each month, 4:00 to 8:00 p.m.
Canadian-American Hall
202 Arlington Street, Watertown, MA 02172

• Set and Ceili Classes
with Sally Harney every Tuesday, 7:30 to 10:00 p.m.
Canadian-American Hall

• Music Classes
every second Saturday
Canadian-American Hall
Sheila Falls, Fiddle
Denis Galvin, Button and Piano Accordion,
Flute, Whistle, Banjo

• Set and Ceili Dancing
with Fergus Keane and Friends
on the fourth Sunday of each month, 4:00 to 8:00 p.m.
Concannon's Village, 60 Lenox Street, Norwood, MA 02062

For more information contact
Larry Reynolds • (617) 899-0911

Comhaltas Ceoltoiri Eireann

Music Organizations

Boston Police Gaelic Column of Pipes and Drums
372 Cornell Street
Boston, MA 02131
Contact: Jim Barry
(617) 327-7875
A 45-member pipes and drums band specializing in Irish pipe music for festivals, parades, concerts, traditional music and performances. Lessons are also available.

Ceol Tradisiúnta na h-Éireann
Contact: Tom Egan
(617) 277-1680
Traditional music club co-founded by the late Billy Caples, RIP. Holds its sessiuns the third Sunday of each month at the VFW Hall, Oak Square, Brighton, from 3:00 p.m. - 7:00 p.m.

Comhaltas Ceoltóirí Éireann
239 Grove Street
Waltham, MA 02154
Contact: Larry Reynolds
(617) 899-0911
Promotes Irish music and Irish culture in all forms through music, singing, dancing and teaching. Holds sessiuns the first Sunday of each month and set dancing every Tuesday night at The Canadian-American Club in Watertown.

Folk Arts Network, Inc.
PO Box 380867
Cambridge, MA 02238
Contact: Stephen Baird
(617) 522-3407 Fax: (617) 522-3407
Community arts, non-profit organization. Publications: Folk Directory and Folk Almanac. Education: Lexington Folk Music School, community music outreach, humano, folk expressions, events and festivals, folk conferences.

Norwood Irish Music Club
90 Wilson Street
Norwood, MA 02062
Jimmy Mawn
(617) 762-7535
Regular music and dance featuring Fergus and Johnny Keane.

Honoring the great Galway musician and showman, whose tune "When Johnny Comes Marching Home" became the anthem of an era.

16 Cedar Terrace
Milton, MA 02184

Contact: Michael Cummings

Patrick S. Gilmore Society
16 Cedar Terrace
Milton, MA 02184
Contact: Michael Cummings
(617) 696-0723
Founded in 1968, the Gilmore Society spreads awareness of the great contribution of "the father of the American concert band." A Galway native, Gilmore wrote such classics as, "When Johnny Comes Marching Home Again." The society meets three times per year and has recently begun to sponsor large scale concerts of marching brass bands that perform at Boston's City Hall Plaza.

Scottish Fiddle Club
Contact: Ed Pearlman
(617) 271-0958
Dedicated to the preservation of Celtic music and culture, with an emphasis on Scottish music. The club holds regular meeetings and conducts dance instructions, music lessons and sessions.

Music Promoters

Garrett Promotions, Inc.
32 College Avenue
Somerville, MA 02144
Contact: Ralph Garrett, Jr.
(617) 666-1536 Fax: (617) 628-0083
Representation of Irish performers: Hal Roach, Phil Coulter, Frank Patterson, Mary McGonigle, Aoife Clancy and Carmel Quinn.

Patrick O'Doherty Management
12 Woodland Street
Belmont, MA 02178
Contact: Patrick Doherty
(617) 489-4840
Music promoters, artist management, concert productions and tour organizers.

Larry Reynolds
239 Grove Street
Waltham, MA 02154
(617) 899-0911
Hosts a number of Irish traditional groups, plus the annual Comhaltas Tour of Champions each October.

Robin Blecher Memorial Fund
535 Concord Avenue
Lexington, MA 02173-8011
Contact: Billie Hockett
Tel/Fax: (617) 862-7837
Celtic concert series. Publishes RBMF Folk Music Conflict Calendar with concerts listed 1 year ahead, up to 700 listings. Compiles concert calendar for Brian O'Donovan's radio program "Celtic Sojourn" on WGBH-89.7 FM.

RADIO PROGRAMS

WACE 730 AM
"Irish Radio Show"
Chicopee
11:00 a.m. to 1:00 p.m. on Saturdays
Contact: Jim Sullivan

WATD 95.9 FM
"Feast of Irish Music"
9:30 a.m. to 5:00 p.m. on Sundays
130 Enterprise Drive
Marshfield, MA 02050
10:00 a.m. to 3:00 p.m. on Sundays
Contact: Seamus Mulligan
(617) 837-4900 Fax: (617) 837-1978

WBET 1460 AM
"Sounds of the Emerald Isle"
Contact: James Larkin/Ellen Larkin
(508) 586-1460

WBRS 100 FM
"The Black Jack Davy Show"
Brandeis University
Waltham, MA 02154
8:00 p.m. to 10:00 p.m. on Mondays
Contact: Andy Nagy
(617) 736-5BRS

WCUW 91.3 FM
"Celtic Connection"
Worcester
9:00 a.m. to 11:00 a.m. Sundays
Contact: Joe McKee
(508) 753-2284

WCUW 91.3 FM
"Four Green Fields"
Worcester
9:30 a.m. to 11:00 a.m. on Saturdays
Contact: Bud Sargent/Des McLoughlin
(508) 753-2284

WEIM AM 1280
"Echoes of Erin"
9:30 a.m. - Noon on Sunday
Contact: Pat McDonagh
(508) 755-1659

THE IRISH RADIO PROGRAM
WNTN 1550 AM

Saturdays, 10:30 a.m. to 7:30 p.m. (or Sundown)

REACHING FROM BOSTON TO LISTENERS IN MAINE, MASSACHUSETTS, NEW HAMPSHIRE AND RHODE ISLAND

YOUR HOSTS
JOHN CURRAN AND BERNIE MCCARTHY

PO Box 12, Belmont, MA 02178
(617) 484-2275/ (617) 326-4159
Fax: (617) 762-4681

WERS 88.9 FM
"Celtic Traditions"
Emerson College, Boston
1:00 p.m. to 3:00 p.m. on Sundays
(617) 578-8892

WGBH 89.7 FM
"A Celtic Sojourn"
Contact: Brian O'Donovan
Sundays from Noon to 2:00 p.m.
(617) 868-9171
The best in traditional and contemporary Irish music.

WICN 90.5 FM
"Thistle & Shamrock"
Worcester
8:00 p.m. - 9:00 p.m. Saturdays
Contact: Fiona Ritchie
(704) 549-9323

WICN 90.5 FM
"Voice of Ireland"
Worcester
8:00 p.m. - 10:00 p.m. on Mondays
Contact: Sean Hastings
(508) 852-6532

WMBR 88.1 FM "Troubador"
MIT, Cambridge
2:00 p.m. to 4:00 p.m. on Thursdays
Contact: Bruce Sylvester
(617) 253-4000

WNTN 1550 AM
"Comhaltas Ceoltóirí Éireann"
10:30 a.m. to Noon on Saturdays
Contact: Larry Reynolds/Sean Reynolds
(617) 899-0911

WNTN 1550 AM
"Sound of Erin"
Contact: John Curran: (617) 484-2275
Contact: Bernie McCarthy
(617) 326-4159
Fax: (617) 762-4681
Noon to Sundown on Saturdays
Up to the minute news, sports, concerts and travel for the greater Bostons Irish community, plus old-time and contemporary Irish music.

WORC AM "Voice of Ireland"
Worcester
8:00 a.m. - 9:00 a.m. on Sundays
Contact: Sean Hastings
(508) 852-6532

WROL Radio 950 AM
"The Irish Hit Parade"
20 Park Plaza, Suite 315
Boston, MA 02116
Contact: Kurt Carbery/Paul Sullivan
(617) 423-0210
10:30 a.m. to 9:00 p.m. on Saturdays
Continuous music, news and sports.

WUMB 91.9 FM
"Celtic Twilight"
U. Mass, Boston
5:00 p.m. to 9:00 p.m. on Saturdays
Contact: Gail Gilmore
(617) 287-6900

WUNR 1600 AM
"Irish Program"
8:00 p.m. to 10:00 p.m. on Thursdays
Contact: Tommy Cummings/
Sheila Cummings
(617) 698-2585

MASSACHUSETTS

WZBC 90.3 FM
"Celtic Program"
5:00 p.m. to 5:30 p.m. on Tuesdays
(617) 552-4686
Boston College's Irish music program.

Record Companies

Beacon Records
PO Box 3129
Peabody, MA 01961
(603) 893-2200
Fax: (603) 893-9441
Beacon Records produces and distributes some of the finest Irish music available, both traditional and contemporary. Inquire at your local record store, or write for a free mail order catalog.

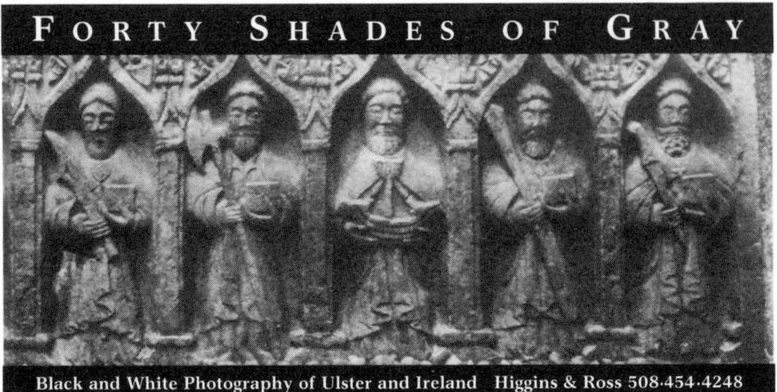

Irish Records International
PO Box 196, Accord Station
Hingham, MA 02018
Contact: Mary Henry/Mattie Henry
(617) 878-7936 Fax: (617) 878-9018
One of the largest distributors in the US and Canada of all the latest Irish cassettes, CD's and videos, as well as old time favorites and traditional Irish music. With a new line of Irish prints, calendars and posters individually signed by famous Irish artist Anne Fitzgerald. The exclusive distributors of all recordings and joke books by Ireland's international comedian Hal Roach.

Rounder Records
1 Camp Street
Cambridge, MA 02140
Contact: Bing Broderick
(617) 354-0700 Fax: (617) 491-1970
Music labels with recordings by Irish artists such as Maura O'Connell, Sharon Shannon, Boys of the Lough and anthologies of Irish music.

Television/ Cable/Videos

Boston Irish Archives
Contact: Katherine Harkins
(617) 328-5503
Video-taping service for Irish events and activities.

Celtic Vision
The Irish Channel
109 Union Wharf
Boston, MA 02109
Contact: Robert Matthews, Dan Leahy, Frank Costello
(617) 367-2888
A newly formed company which brings Irish TV to America 24-hours a day.

Four Provinces
2253 Dorchester Avenue
Dorchester, MA 02124
Contact: Mike McCarron
(617) 296-5519
Video transfer service from Irish to American tapes.

Ireland on the Move
Box 538
Hyde Park, MA 02136
Contact: Tom Clifford
(617) 364-3041
Television program available on Cable TV that covers Irish events and activities in the greater Boston area.

Prestige Photo
392 Hancock Street
North Quincy, MA 02171
(617) 984-0353
Photo processing and international video transfers.

Organizations

Alumni Groups

University College Cork (UCC)
Contact: Martin Spillane
(617) 890-0777

University College Dublin (UCD)
Contact: Nigel Keenan
(617) 723-6443
New England has the largest alumni chapter in the United States.

University College Galway (UCG)
Contact: Katrina Cantrell
(617) 574-0720

Businesses Investments

Boston Ireland Ventures
18 Tremont Street
Suite 147
Boston, MA 02108
Contact: Bill O'Donnell
(617) 723-1361
Boston Ireland Ventures (BIV) is a grassroots charitable effort working to promote jobs, investment and youth training in troubled areas in both communities in Ireland, north and south. Founded in 1987 in Boston, BIV is a non-profit, non-political, tax-exempt organization.

ORGANIZATIONS

Irish Business Network, Inc. (IBN)
44A Harvard Avenue
Brookline, MA 02146
Contact: Una McMahon/John Russell
(617) 731-0794/(617) 665-5604
Fax: (617) 731-4750
IBN, made up of local Irish and Irish-American business people, sponsors many events including seminars, work-shops, trade promotions events and social functions. They also provide a number of services that cater to businesses, trades people, executives and job searchers. Social and educational, career-oriented programs for professionals.

Irish Chamber of Commerce in the USA, Inc. (ICCUSA)
Boston Chapter
167A Washington Street
Norwell, MA 02061
Contact: Thomas Cavanagh
(617) 878-5716
Executive network representing over 300 US and Irish companies. Conducts the Annual Trade Mission to Ireland in May/ June. Provides a complete library of information on doing business between the US and Ireland. Call (203) 877-8131 from your fax/phone to access library.

University College Dublin (UCD)
185 Devonshire Street, #650
Boston, MA 02110
Contact: Robert L. Dey
(617) 350-7779
(617) 350-7860 (fax)
UCD, Ireland's largest university, maintains its North American advancement office in Boston. The UCDNA office provides resources and support for all UCD related activities in North America.

County Clubs

County Donegal Association of Greater Boston
Contact: Mike McCarron:
(617) 696-1702
Mary Ann McGonagle: (617) 665-2083
Hosts regular functions and annual St. Patrick's Day dinner and dance.

County Mayo Association
Emerald Road
Dorchester, MA 02122
Contact: Gerry Curry
(617) 436-4944
Formed in 1985 to promote Irish culture and to provide a social venue for Mayo people.

County Roscommon Association of Boston
2055 Centre Street
West Roxbury, MA 02132
Contact: Richard Gormley
(617) 327-0100
Promotes Irish culture for Roscommon natives and descendants.

Eblana Club of Boston
Dublin Society
57 Walker Street
Newtonville, MA 02160
Contact: Emer Mezzetti
(617) 969-1992
County Dublin society for anybody from Dublin or new arrivals from Ireland to meet and socialize. To promote Irish culture and to establish a regular time and place to assemble with others who are interested in music, dance, history, literature and sports.

Friends of County Clare
PO Box 363
Winchester, MA 01890
Contact: Gerry Dunleavy
(617) 729-8954 Fax: (617) 721-4659
The Friends of County Clare hold an annual social event presenting Irish music with a Clare influence, where immigrants and friends of County Clare get together. All proceeds are donated to charity.

Knights and Ladies of St. Finbarr Corkmen's and Corkwomen's Association
65 Hitty Tom Road
Duxbury, MA 02332
Contact: Dr. William O'Connell
(617) 585-8181
Founded in 1904, the Corkmen's and Corkwomen's club is dedicated to the advancement, enhancement and support of Irish culture with an emphasis on County Cork. Monthly socials are held the second Saturday of each month (not including July and August) at the Knights of Columbus Hall, 15 Winslow Street, Arlington, MA (near Arlington Center). They hold their Annual Banquet during the month of April.

ORGANIZATIONS

St. Brendan's Society
Kerry Social Club
9 Beale Street
Dorchester, MA 02124
Contact: Raymond Walsh
(617) 288-8141
Established in 1904-1905, this Kerry County club promotes Irish culture to members and future members of the Irish-American community through dancing. Coffee, tea and Irish bread served at all socials.

Historical Societies

Irish Mossing Museum
c/o Scituate Historical Society
First Parish Road
Scituate, MA 02066
Contact: Kathleen Laidlaw
(617) 545-1083
This new enterprise is hoping to establish a Museum to display and house history and artifacts, people. Seeking funding and support, it is connected with the gathering, processing and use of Irish moss (carageen) in Scituate. This industry supported Irish immigrants and the town for more than a century.

TIARA
PO Box 619
Sudbury, MA 01776
Contact: Sheila Fitzpatrick
(617) 894-0062
Established in 1983, The Irish Ancestral Research Association (TIARA) is a non-profit organization that develops and promotes the growth, study and exchange of ideas among people interested in Irish genealogical and historical research.

Immigration Services

Immigration and Naturalization Services
JFK Building
Covernment Center
Boston, MA 02203
Contact: Tim Whelan
(617) 565-3879

Irish Immigration Center
18 Tremont Street
Boston, MA 02108
Contact: Lena Deevy
(617) 367-1126 Fax: (617) 367-1420
A non-profit, mainly volunteer-run organization, the IIC works with Irish and non-Irish immigrants to help them adjust to life in the US. Offering assistance in housing, jobs, health care, green cards, social integration with a back-up support network. It offers advice from the many workshops set up to educate people on topics such as citizenship, resumes, job interview skills and anti-racism/multicultural issues. A confidential hotline has also been successfully set up.

Irish Pastoral Centers
The Irish Pastoral Center is a resource and referral agency serving the whole person. Its main purpose is to welcome and support new Irish immigrants by being present and available and providing programs and services to meet their needs.

Irish Pastoral Center
St. Mark's Church
20 Roseland Street
Dorchester, MA 02124
Contact: Fr. Daniel Finn
(617) 436-5436 Fax: (617) 288-9017

Irish Pastoral Center
St. Columbkille's Church
321 Market Street
Brighton, MA 02135
Contact: Fr. Gerry O'Donnell
(617) 562-0219

Irish Pastoral Center
St. Mark's
20 Roseland Street
Dorchester, MA 02124
Contact: Fr. Tim O'Sullivan
(617) 288-2367 Fax: (617) 288-9017

Irish Pastoral Center
28 Billings Road
Quincy, MA 02171
Contact: Sr. Veronica Dobson
(617) 479-7404 Fax: (617) 479-9835

PHILANTHROPY

The American Ireland Fund
211 Congress Street, 10th Floor
Boston, MA 02110
Contact: Kingsley Aikins
(617) 574-0720 Fax: (617) 574-0730
The American Ireland Fund is a non-political, non-sectarian foundation which raises funds in the US for projects promoting the causes of peace, culture and charity in Ireland, North and South. To date, the AIF has raised $50 M for peaceful, constructive change in Ireland, making it the largest private effort of its kind.

Cape Irish Children's Program
PO Box 46
Centerville, MA 02632
Contact: Gerald M. Schulze
(508) 477-3035 Fax: (508) 477-3035
Established in 1975 by clergy and laity of Protestant and Catholic faiths, Cape Irish Children's Program, a non-political, non-sectarian, non-profit, tax exempt organization, wholly made up of volunteers, gives Belfast children a much needed six weeks break on Cape Cod, where they witness first hand different factions living in peace together without fear or prejudice.

Charitable Irish Society
141 Tremont Street
Boston, MA 02111
Contact: Joseph Mulligan/Robert Quinn
(617) 423-3500 Fax: (617) 426-8564
The Charitable Irish Society is the oldest charitable organization in the USA, continuing the original purpose of supporting newly arrived Irish. An annual dinner is held on March 17th.

Emerald Club, Inc.
Box 129, Greendale Station
Worcester, MA 01606
Contact: Walter Conlin - (508) 755-8992
Contact: Cathy Donahue
(508) 755-5944
Formed in 1957 for the sole purpose of supporting the Children of Mercy Center of Worcester, a unique institution catering to persons with developmental disabilities. The Emerald Club organizes an annual fundraising drive for the Center each St. Patrick's season. They also have a summer golf tournament in August and a Half-Way to St. Patrick's Day Party each fall at O'Connor's Restaurant in Worcester.

Friends of the Central Remedial Clinic (CRC)
Boston Chapter, PO Box 201
Boston, MA 02133
Contact: Mary Joyce Morris
(617) 729-0621 Fax: (617) 756-0213
A fund raising group to benefit the Michael Joyce Wing at the Clinic in Dublin, Ireland. The CRC serves all of Ireland and offers services to mentally and physically challenged children and adults. It is a leader in the treatment of its patients and also offers a support system for the family.

Friends of Harvard Celtic Studies
61 Kirkland Street
Cambridge, MA 02138
Contact: Philip Haughey
(617) 496-6305
A group of Harvard alumnus, Irish language enthusiasts and Irish activists dedicated to fundraising on behalf of Harvard's Celtic Studies Program.

Friends of Irish Studies
Boston College
St. Thomas Moore Hall
Chestnut Hill, MA 02167
Contact: Gil Sullivan
(617) 552-4400
Dedicated to strengthening the Irish Studies Program at Boston College through fundraising and by sponsoring cultural activities.

Friends of St. Anne's Cancer Hospital Dublin
17 Alexander Road
Braintree, MA 02184
Contact: Ed Barron
(617) 361-7000
Holds fundraisers for St. Anne's Cancer Hospital Dublin and solicits medical equipment.

The Irish-American Partnership
4 Faneuil Hall Marketplace
Boston, MA 02109
Contact: Mary Sugrue/Joe Leary
(617) 723-2707 Fax: (617) 723-5478
A non-profit organization endorsed by the educational, religious, business and political leaders in Ireland, North and South. Its mission is a strong, healthy, peaceful Ireland through economic development, job creation and education. Activities include a grand Irish auction, golf tournaments, lunches, business seminars, direct mail and travel to Ireland including an executive concierge program.

Irish Georgian Society, Inc. (Mass Chapter)
55 Mount Vernon Street
Boston, MA 02108
Contact: Michael Nagle/William Pear
(617) 227-4045 Fax: (617) 723-7887
With H.Q. in Dublin, this local branch is a non-profit organization that raises funds to send to Ireland for restoration of Irish 18th century heritage. Local lectures and programs are offered to assist in this endeavor.

Political/ Human Rights Groups

American Irish Political Education Committee (PEC)
PO Box 402
Brighton, MA 02135
Contact: James Smith
1-800-777-6807
The PEC is a non-profit organization comprised of American, Irish and non-Irish alike who oppose British Government injustices in Northern Ireland. Seeks a united democratic Ireland, through peaceful means.

Amnesty International USA
58 Day Street
Somerville, MA
(617) 623-0202
A human rights organization which tracks government violations around the world. Has issued numerous reports on Northern Ireland.

Boston Three Defense Fund
PO Box 864
Boston, MA 02103
Contact: Kathleen O'Brien
(617) 552-6600

Citizens for the MacBride Principles
Contact Dick OhEigertaigh
(617) 327-0231
An ad hoc committee formed to enact tougher MacBride legislation.

Committee for a New Ireland
c/o 294 Washington Street
Boston, MA 02108
Contact: Michael Donlan
(617) 482-1360 Fax: (617) 556-3890
CNI works to promote peace and reconciliation amongst the Irish people North and South, especially between the two sectarian communities, working with their political leaders and human rights groups.

Irish-American Labor Coalition of New England
AFL-CIO
8 Beacon Street
Boston, MA 02108
Contact: Marty Foley
(617) 696-1479
The Labor Coalition is a powerful national group of labor activists who have developed a better understanding among Americans of the conditions in Northern Ireland through education and lobbying activities. The New England branch has helped lead the effort on the MacBride Principles, making Massachusetts the first state to approve the Principles. More recently, it successfully lobbied to bring Sinn Féin leader, Gerry Adams, to New York to discuss conditions in Northern Ireland.

MASSACHUSETTS

Irish National Caucus
5 Leggs Hill Road
Marblehead, MA 01945
Contact: Leo Cooney/Anne Cooney
(617) 631-1363
A non-violent human rights organization dedicated to getting America to stand up for human rights in Ireland. The Irish National Caucus initiated, proposed and launched the MacBride Principles - a corporate code of conduct for US companies doing business in Northern Ireland. National headquarters is located in Washington, DC (202) 544-0568.

Irish Northern Aid Committee
New England Regional Office
24 King Street
Swampscott, MA 01907
Contact: Joe McHugh
(617) 598-6228
INA is the oldest and largest organization in the US, dedicated exclusively to aiding the Nationalist victims of the Anglo-Irish conflict. The families of nearly 1,000 prisoners in five countries rely upon the dedication of volunteers to fund-raise across America on behalf of An Cuman Cabhrach and Green Cross, prisoner assisted trusts based in Ireland since the 1950's. INA works with Irish-Americans and human and civil rights groups to promote an end to conflict, to aid the release of prisoners and to end British occupation of six counties in Ireland.

Irish Northern Aid
Box 864
Boston, MA 02103
Contact: Kathleen O'Brien
(617) 552-6600

Religious Groups

Irish Holy Ghost Fathers' Mission
Contact: Fr. Peter Nolan
(617) 325-1300

"Make it Known" with Fr. Pat
PO Box 238
Attleboro, MA 02703
Contact: Fran Gunning
(617) 551-9200 Fax: (617) 551-0087
Make it known is a healing ministry with services monthly at LaSalette Shrine in Attleboro. Fr. Pat is a well known singer and has released fourteen tapes and five video tapes which include three featuring Ireland.

Social Clubs

Ancient Order of Hibernians
The AOH was organized on May 4, 1836 in New York City. It played a pivotal role in helping Irish immigrants adjust to American society during the 19th century. Today the men's and women's branches of the AOH are active across the country promoting Irish culture, contributing to American values, Christian charity, the Catholic Church, supporting issues in Ireland and Northern Ireland and promoting friendship and unity within the organization. The Massachusetts divisions are as follows:

State President
John Meehan
19 Upcrest Road
Brighton, MA 02135
(617) 254-8528

George Thomas
President Essex County Board
11 Marc Lane
Lawrence, MA 01843

Michael McCarthy
President of Middlesex County Board
1150 Fellsway Road
Malden, MA 02148

Michael Carroll
President Worcester County Board
12 Marsh Avenue
Worcester, MA 02605
(508) 852-1418

Rev. James Champion
Deputy National Chaplain
48 St. Paul Street
Blackstone, MA 01504
(508) 883-6726

Division 1
Daniel Curran
51 Meadowview Road
Holyoke, MA 01040

Division 1
Gerald Deeley
PO Box 614
Franklin, MA 02038
(413) 536-1895

Division 1
Michael Ferrick
6 Bromfield
Newburyport, MA 01950
(508) 462-9804

ORGANIZATIONS

Division 1
Michael Joyce
PO Box 622
Manomet, MA 02345
(508) 224-3253

Division 1
Albert Madden
PO Box 33
Boston, MA 02122
(617) 288-4938

Division 6
Robert Flaherty
150 M. Street
South Boston, MA 02127
(617) 464-3165

Division 7
Peter McCoy
41 Vine Street
New Bedford, MA 02740
(508) 994-3126

Division 8
William Sullivan
201 Bailey Street
Lawrence, MA 01843
(508) 682-4875

Division 8
Michael Ward
10 Rigby Place
Clinton, MA 01510
(508) 368-3243

Division 10
David Johansen
13 Hawthorne Street
Lynn, MA 01902
(617) 592-8177

Division 11
Paul Peterson
58 Crescent Street
Lynnfield, MA 01940
(617) 334-3808

Division 12
David McCleary
39 Gaston Road
Medford, MA 02155
(617) 324-9250

Division 14
John Cranitch
Box 146 - Newton Branch
Boston, MA 02258
(617) 923-0405

Division 16
John Ryan
18 Ringold Street
Marlboro, MA 01752
(508) 481-1175

Division 17
Louis Ballou
28 Pacheco Drive
North Smithfield, RI 02895
(401) 766-4181

Division 18
Michael Slaven
29 Hanson Street
Salem, MA 01970
(508) 741-3783

Division 19
Angus MacDonald
284 Wheeler Street
Dracut, MA 01852
(508) 453-8580

INCORPORATED

Organized in New York City, May 4, 1836

Proud of your Irish heritage? And Catholic faith? Concerned about human rights violations in Northern Ireland? Join the AOH today. You'll meet people interested in and knowledgeable about Irish culture and history.

The AOH dates back to the 16th century. As a member, you'll receive The National Hibernian Digest, a publication which provides interesting, thoughtful articles on Irish culture, history and lifestyle. For information on joining or starting an AOH division in your area, please contact any of the following:

Jack Meehan, State President: (617) 254-8528
Jack Lawless, Vice-President: (508) 535-8023
Joe Healy, Secretary: (508) 465-2054
Jack Hatch, Treasurer: (508) 532-0572
Mike Joyce, State Organizer: (508) 224-3253

A special invitation is extended to members of the new Irish community of Boston.

Division 32
Paul Doyle
54 Jaffrey Street
Weymouth, MA 02189
(617) 331-5188

Division 36
Brother Thomas Fahey
378 Main Street
Shrewsbury, MA 01545
(508) 845-1875

Billerica Irish-American Club, Inc.
616 Middlesex Turnpike
PO Box 845
Billerica, MA 01865
Contact: Deirdre Leger
(508) 667-3762
With its own in-house catering and wait staff, the Billerica Irish-American Club kitchen caters to banquets, weddings, showers and other functions for the Irish-American community. A full menu is served Friday evenings from 5:30 p.m. to 9:30 p.m. for members and their guests, along with top Irish bands in the pub section starting at 8:30 p.m. Along with live music and dance they also hold an annual festival. (See Annual Events section).

Boston Rose of Tralee Pageant
171 Waverly Street
Arlington, MA 02174
Contact: Eileen O'Sullivan
(617) 643-6694
This annual event to promote Irish culture and heritage for girls of Irish descent aged from 19-25. They are judged on poise, personality, intelligence, graciousness and good dress sense. Contests start March through May with the grand final held in June. The lucky finalist wins a trip to Ireland for 10 days.

The Boston Yeats Society
c/o McCormick Bowers Associates, Inc.
14 Beacon Street, Room 606
Boston, MA 02135
Contact: Jane Bowers
(617) 742-7292 Fax: (617) 720-2765
While the Boston Yeats Society's interests include all Irish literature, drama and poetry, its primary focus is on the life and writings of W. B. Yeats. Events include lectures by Yeats scholars (i.e. Helen Vendler); poetry readings by such poets as Seamus Heaney and Connie Veenendaal and other performances and social events relating to Yeats.

Éire Society of Boston
23 Hunters Ridge Road
Concord, MA 01742
Contact: T. Fitzgerald, Jr.
(617) 742-4700 Fax: (617) 742-4791
The Éire Society was organized some sixty years ago for the purpose of spreading the awareness of the cultural achievements of the Irish people.

Emerald Society of the Boston Police, Inc.
10 Birch Street
Roslindale, MA 02131
Contact: Emmett McNamara
(617) 323-9018
Organized to develop a spirit of brotherhood amongst its members and to promote the Gaelic culture. An awards banquet is held annually. Their function hall is available for rent and can hold up to 130 people.

Fitchburg Irish-American Association
31 Ward Street
Fitchburg, MA 01420
Contact: James Cleary
(508) 342-3797
An Irish-American organization whose members have traceable Irish ancestry. Dedicated to the preservation and promotion of Irish cultural heritage. Promoters of the first annual Irish Festival in Massachusetts in 1980, and the originators of the Irish festivals in Massachusetts.

Friendly Sons of St. Patrick
PO Box J4021
New Bedford, MA 02740
Contact: Richard H. Brown, Sr.
(508) 996-1569
The Friendly Sons of St. Patrick provide scholarships to needy students and give donations to city and statewide organizations in need of help. Their aim is to promote ethnic culture in the community.

Irish-American Club of Malden
177 West Street
Malden, MA
Contact: Ed Norton
(617) 321-7720
Social club hosting charity functions, cultural programs.

Irish-American Cultural Institute
Contact: Michael Dwyer
(617) 326-1977
The IACI is at the forefront of promoting Irish culture and achievements. Programs include high school exchange courses, tree plantings, lecture tours and scholarships.

Irish-American Veterans of Massachusetts
Contact: Jack Doherty
(617) 327-0011
This group of Irish-American veterans is dedicated to promoting its contribution to America's armed forces.

MASSACHUSETTS

The Irish Club
564 Milbury Street
Worcester, MA 01610
(508) 792-0922
Irish entertainment each weekend. Dancing classes for children.

The Irish Cultural Center
1895 Center Street, Suite 7
West Roxbury, MA 02132
Contact: Judy Collins
(617) 323-3399 Fax: (617) 323-8006
The Irish Cultural Center represents the coming together of the Irish community in the greater Boston area to establish a center that will promote and preserve Irish culture. It is a non-political, non-partisan and non-profit organization. Their annual Irish Festival week-end is held in June at Stonehill College.

Irish Social Club of Boston
119 Park Street
West Roxbury, MA 02132
(617) 327-7306
Formed in 1945, the Irish Social Club has nearly 2,000 members. The club conducts weekly dances, plus music, language and dance lessons. Hosts the annual Leo C. McDevitt Memorial Golf Invitational Tournament each June.

John Boyle O'Reilly Club
33 Progress Avenue
Springfield, MA
Contact: Larry Griffin
(413) 739-2865
Dedicated to the memory of O'Reilly, the famed poet, rebel and social reformer. The club has over 1200 members and holds regular functions.

The Kingdom Social Club
4 Allen Place
Melrose, MA 02176
Contact: Noreen McDonnell
(617) 878-4039
A young, growing, Irish social club, whose members get together at functions to meet old and new friends.

St. Brendan's Society
9 Beale Street
Dorchester, MA 02124
Contact: Raymond Walsh
(617) 288-8141
Established in 1904-1905, this Kerry social club promotes Irish culture to members and future members of the Irish-American community through dancing. Coffee, tea and Irish bread served at all socials.

TIARA
PO Box 619
Sudbury, MA 01776
Contact: Sheila Fitzpatrick
(617) 894-0062
Established in 1983, The Irish Ancestral Research Association (TIARA) is a non-profit organization that develops and promotes the growth, study and exchange of ideas among people interested in Irish genealogical and historical research.

ORGANIZATIONS

Other

Boston Firefighters Local 718
55 Hallet Street
Dorchester, MA 02124
Contact: James Fitzgerald
(617) 288-2100 Fax: (617) 288-2090

Pubs/ Restaurants

Irish Food Products

Adams Corner General Store
776 Adams Street, Adams Village
Dorchester, MA 02125
(617) 282-6370
Irish candies and food products.

Bread 'N Bits of Ireland
530 Main Street
Melrose, MA 02176
Contact: Mary Anne McGonagle
(617) 662-5800
Irish bakery.

Conlon's Market
Ashmont Street
Dorchester, MA 02125
Contact: John Flaherty
Irish food products and meats.

Greenhills Traditional Irish Bakery
793 Adams Street
Dorchester, MA 02124
Cynthia Quinn/Dermot Quinn
(617) 825-8187
Baked fresh daily, all home-made Irish breads, cakes, pastries and scones. Variety of imported Irish groceries and chocolates.

Keltic Krust
1371 Washington Street
West Newton, MA
(617) 332-9343
Full line of fresh baked Irish goods. Closed on Mondays.

McGowan's Corner Store
1658 Dorchester Ave. at Center St.
Dorchester, MA 02125
Contact: Bill McGowan
Irish food products and meats.

O'Driscoll's Fresh Butchers
Time Square Plaza
299 West Haven Street
Northborough, MA 01532
Contact: Michael O'Driscoll
(508) 393-2064 Fax: (508) 393-2401
Meat and deli seafood specialties. Irish papers including The Irish Reporter.

Patrick Nee Irish Imports
(508) 583-2213
Distributes Shannon traditional foods, Galtee bacon, sausage and black and white pudding. Retail and food services available.

Shamrock Foods Exports Ltd.
35 Somerset Avenue
Winthrop, MA 02152
Contact: Rich Currier
(617) 846-3012 Fax (617) 846-4616
Shamrock is a full line supplier of imported Irish grocery products covering categories such as teas, preserves, marmalades, bread mixes, cereals, mustards, fruit cakes and Irish smoked salmon.

Pubs/ Restaurants

The Abbey
448 West Second Street
South Boston, MA 02127
(617) 268-4100
Live music every Thursday and Sunday night.

Bay Tower Room
60 State Street
Boston, MA 02109
(617) 723-1668
(617) 723-7887 (fax)
One of the best views of Boston, caterss to numerous Irish functions.

Bayside Club
367 East Eighth Street
South Boston, MA 02127
(617) 269-1640
Food and entertainment, plus special activities like the annual St. Patrick's Day breakfast hosted by Senate President William Bulger.

Bean Pot Grill & Sports Bar
150 Canal Street
Boston, MA 02114
(617) 722-9321
Next to the Boston Garden. Giant sports screens.

The Black Rose
160 State Street
Boston, MA
(617) 742-2286
Rousing ballads and singalongs, lunch served daily.

The Black Rose
50 Church Street
Harvard Square
Cambridge, MA
(617) 492-8630
Jazz, rock, Irish, plus extensive menu.

Blackthorn Pub
471 West Broadway
South Boston, MA 02127
Contact: Frank Gillespie
(617) 269-1159
Music on weekends, sporting matches regularly shown.

The Blarney Stone
1509 Dorchester Avenue
Fields Corner
Dorchester, MA 02122
(617) 825-8877
The Boston Globe calls it "a throwback to when Fields Corner was a transplanted Irish County. The waitresses are prompt and agreeable, the stout, marvelous."

The Boyne Pub & Restaurant
458 Western Avenue
Brighton, MA 02135
Contact: Conor Hoey
(617) 782-2418
Live Irish music Friday and Saturday nights. Irish breakfast served Saturdays and Sundays. Three TV's and large screen available.

Brendan Behan Pub
378A Centre Street
Hyde Square
Jamaica Plain, MA 02130
(617) 522-5386
Traditional sessions every Tuesday night and Saturday afternoon plus poetry readings and Irish theater regularly.

Buck Mulligan's Pub
1732 Centre Street
West Roxbury, MA 02132
Contact: Joe Greene
(617) 323-9572

Cape Cod Claddagh Inn and Tavern
77 Main Street (Route 28)
West Harwich, MA 02671
Contact: Eileen Connell/Jack Connell
(508) 432-9628
1-800-356-9628 for reservations
Irish hospitality in a Victorian ambience. Full service B&B Inn that serves Irish breakfast with an Irish pub, restaurant and art gallery. Sessions on Saturday nights feature Pat and Kay O'Brien, accordion, Mike Soles, guitar and vocals and Seamus Healy on whistle & boudhrán. Call for a free brochure.

Cape Cod Irish Village
512 Main Street, Rt. 28
West Yarmouth, MA 02673
Contact: Alan Delaney/Tom Davis
(508) 771-0100 Fax: (508) 771-3305
The Irish Village is an 88 unit motor lodge located on Cape Cod. Irish entertainment is performed each evening along with tempting Irish dishes as well as regular fare for breakfast and dinner.

Castlebar
575 Washington Street
Brighton, MA 02135
Contact: Paul Clougher
(617) 783-5722

The Cellar
911 Massachusetts Avenue
Cambridge, MA 02138
Contact: Marilyn Carter
(617) 876-2580

The Center Village Pub
1664 Dorchester Avenue
Dorchester, MA 02124
Contact: Dennis Queally

Century Irish Pub
29 Locust Street
Falmouth, MA 02540
Contact: Sharon Fackos/Jay Kenney
(508) 548-6631
The Cape's oldest Irish pub offers live Irish entertainment seven nights a week with happy hour entertainment every Friday, Saturday and Sunday afternoon.

Claddagh Inn
Route 102
West Stockbridge, MA 01266
Contact: Barbara and Jack O'Neill
(413) 232-7092
Small elegant inn in the Berkshires with Irish hospitality, including Irish breakfast.

Claddagh Restaurant
113 Dartmouth Street
Boston, MA 02118
(617) 262-9874
Traditional Irish food, music evenings, function room.

Brendan Behan Pub

378 Centre Street
Jamaica Plain/Boston, MA 02130
(617) 522-5386
(617) 232-1736

The Cellar

Where the Staff is Friendly,
The Conversation is Intelligent, and
The Pints Are Perfect.

911 Massachusetts Avenue
(Between Harvard and Central Squares)
Cambridge, MA 02138
(617) 876-2580

Chelsea Tap Bar
802 Broadway
Chelsea, MA
Contact: Bart Galvin
(617) 884-8995

Concannon's Irish Village
60 Lenox Street
Norwood, MA 02062
Contact: Thomas Concannon
(617) 762-3610
Public lounge, function room with a capacity of 400 to host all types of parties and weddings. Dancing every Saturday night.

The Corrib Pub
396 Market Place
Brighton, MA 02135
(617) 787-0882

Deeney O'Malley's Pub
East Broadway
South Boston, MA 02127
Contact: Phil Deeney/Peter O'Malley
(617) 269-0976
Entertainment Thursday through Sunday evenings. Two fireplaces.

Doyle's Restaurant
3484 Washington Street
Jamaica Plain, MA 02130
Contact: Jerry Burke
(617) 524-2345
Established in 1882, Doyle's is a neighborhood gathering place frequented by politicians, students and media types. Great food and entertainment.

The Druid Pub
1357 Cambridge Street
Inman Square
Cambridge, MA 02139
Contact: Peter Smyth
(617) 491-1256
(617) 497-0956
Late afternoon sessions on Saturdays and Sundays. Live, unplugged music, storytelling, dancing and poetry. Unique Irish sculptures and paintings add to the festive yet peaceful atmosphere.

Dubliner Pub
197 Market Street
Lowell, MA
(508) 458-2120
Irish music, dining. No cover charge.

The Eire Pub
795 Adams Street
Adams Village
Dorchester, MA 02122
Pay phone.

The Eire Pub of Roslindale
635 Hyde Park Avenue
Roslindale, MA
(617) 323-9616

Emerald Isle
Milbury Street
Worcester, MA
Contact: Martin Patton/Margaret Patton
(508) 754-7676
Fine dining available.

Emerald Isle Bar & Lounge
1501 Dorchester Avenue
Dorchester, MA 02124
Contact: Margaret Nellany
(617) 288-0010
Live entertainment Thursday through Saturday - 9:30 p.m. to 1:30 a.m.

Flann O'Brien's Pub
1619 Tremont Street
Brigham Circle
Mission Hill, MA
Contact: Finbar (Butch) Murray
(617) 566-4148
Great food, music, frequented by Irish immigrants, students and the local medical center staff.

Gerard's Restaurant
776 Adams Street
Dorchester, MA 02124
(617) 282-6370
Full Irish breakfast Saturdays and Sundays.

The Green Briar
304 Washington Street
Brighton, MA 02135
Contact: Austin O'Connor
(617) 789-4100
Brighton's Irish restaurant and pub offers a wide variety of appetizers, lunch and dinner selections. It features great local bands and Boston's finest Irish session every Monday night.

The Green Dragon Tavern
11 Marshall Street
Boston, MA
Contact: John Somers
(617) 367-0055 Fax: (617) 350-0004
The Green Dragon on Boston's Freedom Trail, Boston's newest Irish pub has for its theme, the part the Irish played in the American Revolution. In 1775 the bar was known as "A Nest of Treason." Lunch seven days a week, music most evenings, and Irish traditional sessions Saturday afternoons.

Harp at the Garden
85 Causeway Street
Boston, MA 02114
Contact: Des Kearns
(617) 742-1010
Downtown's newest Irish restaurant and pub features a complete lunch and dinner menu along with some of Boston's best live bands. Try their, all-you-can-eat Sunday Jazz Brunch, or the all-you-can-eat lunch buffet.

Irish Embassy Pub
234 North Friend Street
(near Boston Garden)
Boston, MA 02114
Contact: Tommy McGann/Joe Dunne
(617) 742-6618
Live entertainment seven nights a week, featuring international and local acts.

1882 Irish Embassy
502 Foundry Street
South Easton, MA
(508) 238-1882
Featuring top traditional and contemporary Irish music, fine Irish cuisine.

Irish Village
224 Market Street
Brighton, MA 02135
Contact: Peter Lee
(617) 787-5427
Lunch served daily.

Iron Horse Music Hall
20 Center Street
Northampton, MA
1-800-The-Tick
Features top Irish and Celtic performers throughout the year.

J. J. Foley's Cafe
117 E. Berkeley Street
Boston, MA
Contact: Jerry Foley
Frequented by Herald reporters, City Hall workers and trolley operators.

Jose McIntyre's
160 Milk Street
Boston, MA 02109
(617) 451-9460
Mexican meals in an Irish setting. Lunch and dinner, function room.

The Kells
161 Brighton Avenue
Allston, MA 02134
Contact: Gerry Quinn/John McClure
(617) 782-9082
Entertainment seven nights a week, featuring the region's top Irish musicians. This is the home of Boston's World Cup Soccer network. Their function room holds up to 200 people with fine food available.

Kelly's Square Pub
13 Kelly Square
East Boston, MA 02128
(617) 567-4627

The Kinvara Pub
34 Harvard Avenue
Allston, MA 02134
Contact: Austin O'Connor, Jr.
(617) 783-9400
This Allston pub offers great appetizers and a complete lunch and dinner menu, including weekly dinner specials for just $1.99. The Kinvara also offers fine pints and features the best local bands.

Liam's Irish Tavern
1 Framingham Circle
Framingham, MA
Contact: Bill Haughey
(508) 875-6114

Limerick's
34 Batterymarch Street
Boston, MA
(617) 350-7975

Littlest Bar
49 Province Street
Boston, MA
Contact: Paddy Grace
(617) 523-9766
Boston's tiniest pub, located near the Boston Common.

Molly Malone's
Sheraton Tara Hotel
37 Forbes Road
Braintree, MA 02184
Contact: Barry Storey
(617) 848-2000 Fax: (617) 843-9492
Molly Malone's features Irish entertainment five nights a week, Tuesday through Saturday. Molly's also offers complimentary hors d'oeuvres, an authentic Irish menu and barside darts. Plenty of free parking available.

Molly Malone's
Sheraton Tara Hotel
1657 Worcester Road
Framingham, MA 01701
Contact: Donogh McCarthy
(508) 879-2900 Fax (508) 875-7593
Molly Malone's offers five nights of entertainment Tuesday through Saturday. Complimentary hors d'oeuvres are served along with an authentic Irish menu, darts and a pool table. Free parking available.

Mr. Dooley's Boston Tavern
77 Broad Street
Boston, MA
Contact: Michael Sherlock
(617) 338-9171
Kitchen open daily, 11:00 a.m. - 9:00 p.m. Voted Best of Boston, Best Irish Breakfast, served every Sunday 11:00 a.m. to 5:00 p.m., followed by "Ceili House" with Alan Loughnane, 6:00 p.m. to 11:00 p.m. Sessions every Tuesday, Wednesday and Thursday night with Shea Walker and Alan Loughnane. Pub Quiz Monday night.

My Honey Fitz "Irish Pub"
142 Pleasant Street
Malden, MA 02148
Contact: Jimmy Sullivan
(617) 324-0111
An Irish pub with entertainment Thursday through Saturday. Guinness, Harp and Bass available on tap with lunch, dinner and function rooms.

Nash's Pub
1154 Dorchester Avenue
Dorchester, MA 02124
Contact: Pete Nash
(617) 436-4134
Home of Kerry football club.

Noel Henry's Emerald Room
Cape Codder Hotel
Route 132 and Bearse's Way
Hyannis, MA 02601
Contact: Noel Henry
(508) 790-4348 Fax: (508) 771-6564
Noel Henry's Emerald Room features the biggest names in Irish entertainment. It also features an oversized dance floor, grill menu, and is fully air conditioned. Overnight packages are available at the Cape Codder Hotel.

Nostalgia
797 Quincy Shore Drive
Quincy, MA
Contact: Jim McGettrick
(617) 479-8989
Irish pub with restaurant, night club, bands, performers, dancers, storytellers and an annual concert.

THE GREEN DRAGON TAVERN

"The Headquarters of the American Revolution"

Traditional Boston Tavern Fare
Live Entertainment 6 Nights a Week
Located on Boston's Freedom Trail

11 MARSHALL STREET, BOSTON

(617) 367-0055

Mr. Dooley's Boston Tavern

"A Great Place For A Pint And A Chat"
As seen in Condé Nast Traveler

Live Irish Music
6 nights a week

Imported Beers
on draft

Kitchen open
11 am-9 pm daily

77 Broad Street • Boston • MA 02109
(617) 338 • 5656

Traditional Irish Breakfast every Sunday 11am to 5pm

O'Connor's Restaurant & Bar
1160 W. Boylston Street
Worcester, MA
Contact: Brendan O'Connor
Clare O'Connor
(508) 853-0789
Fine Irish restaurant dining, an authentic Irish newly renovated pub and function rooms. This is the local Irish gathering place and is used to celebrate breakfast events and parade events. This establishment also sponsors many local Irish Worcester events.

Old Irish Ale House
Routes 1 and 109
Dedham, MA 02026
Contact: Tony Haggarty
(617) 329-6034
Elegant dining, especially the new Waterford Place function room. Irish music throughout the week, from ceili and Irish folk to top 40 and oldies.

The Old Timer Restaurant
155 Church Street
Clinton, MA 01510
Contact: James McNally
(508) 365-5980
Located at the sign of the shamrock, this traditional Irish-owned family restaurant has been thriving for over sixty years. Sunday evenings finds The Jug O'Punch performing from 4:00 p.m. to 8:00 p.m. (except July and August). Chef and owner, Jim McNally, an Irish tenor, also performs Wednesdays and weekends.

O'Leary's Pub
1010 Beacon Street
Brookline, MA 02146
Contact: Angus O'Leary
(617) 734-0049
Fine Irish cooking, Irish traditional session late Sunday afternoons.

Paddy Burke's Pub
132 Portland Street
Boston, MA 02114
Contact: Ned Giblin
(617) 367-8370
Lunches, live music, giant sports screen.

Pat Flanagan's Pub and Grill
79 Parking Way
Quincy, MA 02169
(617) 773-3400

Plough & Stars Pub
912 Massachusetts Avenue
Cambridge, MA 02138
Contact: George Crowley
(617) 492-9653
Lunches daily, music nightly.

Purple Shamrock
1 Union Street
Boston, MA
(617) 227-2060
Located next to Quincy Market, the Shamrock has live music several nights a week. Serves lunch and dinner.

Sabina Doyle's Restaurant
116 Main Street, Route 109
Medway, MA
(508) 533-1343

Stadium Pub (Boyne)
458 Western Avenue
Allston, MA 02134
(617) 782-2418

Tara Room
1921 Dorchester Ave.
Dorchester, MA 02125
(617) 282-5637

Triple D's Restaurant and Pub
435 South Huntington Avenue
Jamaica Plain, MA 02130
Contact: Tom DeCourcy /Joe Devlin
(617) 720-0166
Local pub, hot meals served.

Twelve Bens Pub
315 Adams Street
Dorchester, MA 02122
(617) 265-6727
Kitchen open daily from 11:30 a.m. to 6:30 p.m. Live music on weekends.

West Roxbury Pub
1883 Centre Street
West Roxbury, MA 02132
(617) 469-2624

NOBODY'S MORE IRISH THAN NOEL AND MOLLY.

For the most authentic Irish entertainment and atmosphere, **Tara Hotels** gives you two great choices: Noel Henry's Emerald Room and Molly Malone's Irish Entertainment Taverns.

Noel Henry's, located in the Cape Codder Hotel on Cape Cod, features the biggest names in Irish entertainment, with overnight packages available. Molly Malone's, at the **Sheraton Tara Hotels** in Framingham and Braintree, MA, offers an authentic Irish menu, Irish performers and free hors d'oeuvres.

When only the best Irish entertainment will do, Noel Henry's Emerald Room and Molly Malone's are the perfect couple. ♣

Sheraton Tara Hotel
1657 Worcester Rd. • Framingham, MA
(508) 879-7200

Sheraton Tara Hotel
37 Forbes Rd. • Braintree, MA
(617) 848-0600

A TARA® HOTEL/THE FLATLEY COMPANY

Rt. 132 & Bearse's Way • Hyannis, MA
(508) 771-3000

Services

Airlines (Ireland & Great Britain)

Aer Lingus
1-800-223-6537

American Airlines
1-800-433-7300

American Trans Air
Call you local travel agent.

British Airways
1-800-247-9297

Delta Airlines
1-800-221-1212

Northwest Airlines
1-800-447-4747

Pan American Airlines
1-800-221-1111

Tower Air
Call your local travel agent.

US Air
1-800-428-4322

Virgin Atlantic Airlines
1-800-862-8621

Beauty Salons

Hair Care
116 Dorchester Street
South Boston, MA 02127
(617) 268-6868

Talking Heads
1766 Dorchester Avenue
Dorchester, MA 02124
(617) 265-2274

Books

Ford and Bailie Publishers/ Distributors
PO Box 138
Belmont, MA 02178
Contact: Chadine Bailie
(617) 489-6635 Fax: (617) 489-6388
Celtic books for scholars and students.

Globe Corner Bookstore
One School Street
Boston, MA 02108
Contact: Pat Carrier
(617) 723-1676
Stocks travel and local Irish books.

Steve Griffin
9 Irvington Road
Medford, MA 02155
(617) 396-8440
Distributes over 2,500 books on Celtic topics and languages.

Waterstone's Booksellers
Cnr. Newbury and Exeter Streets
Boston, MA 02115
Contact: Bert Wright
(617) 859-7300
One of Boston's finest bookstores features a substantial section of Irish history and literature. Featuring readings and signings at the store by authors like Seamus Heaney, Roddy Doyle, P. J. Donleavy, Derek Mahon and more.

SERVICES

BUSINESSES

Concept Group
15 Depot Square
Lexington, MA 02173
Contact: Susan Burke
(617) 674-0137 Fax: (617) 674-2080
Concept Group consults on a wide range of marketing and export-related topics, (both for small US companies and Irish companies wishing to enter the US market).

Enterprise Consulting Group
73 Parker Road
Needham, MA 02194
Contact: Louise Reilly Sacco
(617) 444-6631
(617) 444-6757 (fax)
Consultants for small Irish businesses.

Ireland's Coins
Box 833
Scituate, MA 02066
Contact: Mr. Donahue
(617) 545-3269
Mail order company.

Katherine Kane, Inc.
59 Temple Place, Suite 608
Boston, MA 02111
Contact: Marybeth Mackay
(617) 338-2288 Fax: (617) 338-6885
Special events, conferences and tours, public relations and promotions for national and international business programs.

Peter Kimmons
(617) 924-1092
Limo Service, Greater Boston.

McGowan Associates
1658 Dorchester Avenue
Dorchester, MA 02122
Contact: Bill McGowan
(617) 265-9545
Accounting and insurance.

Terence McCarthy
(617) 661-4351
Locksmith, safes opened and changed, locks and door closes installed.

O'Brien Associates, Inc.
59 Temple Place, Suite 602
Boston, MA 02111
Contact: Colum O'Brien
(617) 426-0533 Fax: (617) 426-6564
Permanent placement agency dealing exclusively with mutual fund organizations. Requires candidates who have experience in this area.

Frank Pluck
Electrical Services
219 Harvard Street
Cambridge, MA 02139
(617) 876-5476

Repele of New England, Inc.
168 Neponset Street, #4
Canton, MA 02021
Contact: Terry O'Brien
(617) 821-2555
Cleaning and stain protection of carpets, upholstery and drapes in both residential and commercial areas. Daily cleaning of office buildings - 24 hour service.

Signs Unique
25 Thomsow Street
Winchester, MA 01890
Contact: Patricia O'Neill
(617) 721-1325

The Tax Doctor
21 Hunnewell Avenue
Brighton, MA 02135
Contact: Dónal Keane
(617) 789-4931
Expert advice and help in the preparation of taxes. Free consultation and estimates. Specializing in personal, small business and new immigrant tax preparation.

Gift Shops

Aisling Gallery
229 Lincoln Street
Hingham, MA 02043
Contact: Maureen and John Connolly
(617) 749-0555
Original Irish art and gifts.

Boreen Irish Imports
9 Boston Street
Lynn, MA 01904
(617) 598-9286

Bread N' Bits of Ireland
530 Main Street
Melrose, MA 02176
Contact: Mary Anne McGonagle
(617) 662-5800

Bridgets - An Irish Tradition
Cordage Park Marketplace
Plymouth, MA 02360
(508) 747-2273

Bridgets - An Irish Tradition
The Mall at Walpole
Walpole, MA 02032
(508) 747-7904

Cape Cod Irish Village
512 Main Street
West Yarmouth, MA 02673
(508) 771-0100

Celtic Corner at Leary's
202 Merrimac Street
Newburyport, MA 01950
Contact: Marybeth Finnegan
(508) 462-4451 Fax: (508) 462-4452
A full line Irish gift shop featuring apparel, jewelry, pottery, china, books and music. Irish food products such as sausages, rashers, black and white puddings and tea also available.

Celtic Origins
The Curtis Shops at Walker Street
Lenox, MA 01240
(413) 637-1296

Celtic Weavers
Fanueil Hall Marketplace
Boston, MA 02109
Contact: Richard Senier
(617) 720-0750
Offers high quality Irish goods, including name brand clothing, Celtic jewelry, and a wide selection of Irish music and tapes.

Emerald Isle Imports
Harbor Light Mall
Route 3A
North Weymouth, MA 02091
(617) 447-0469

Emerald Isle Imports
11 School Street
Quincy, MA 02169
(617) 447-0469

THE IRISH COTTAGE

DISTINCTIVE IMPORTS

A Unique Gift Shop
Featuring A Wide Range of Gifts with
an Irish and European Flavor!

Irish Cassettes and Videos
Waterford and Galway Crystals
Complete Range of Claddagh Jewelry
Belleek, Donegal and Royal Tara Chinas
Handknit Sweaters, Hats, Caps & Mittens
AND A WHOLE LOT MORE . . .

South Shore Plaza, Braintree .... (617) 848-8609
Dedham Mall, Dedham .... (617) 326-6525
Burlington Mall, Burlington .... (617) 272-1044
Royal Ridge Mall, Nashua, NH .... (603) 888-4368
Garden City Center, Cranston, R.I. .... (401) 943-0282
Hanover Mall, Hanover .... (617) 829-0098

"North America's Largest Specialty Irish Retailer"

We Advertise On:

"Feast of Irish Music"

Sunday 10 a.m. to 1 p.m. • WATD • 95.9 FM

Erin's Own Irish Imports
174 Elm Street
Westfield, MA 01085
Contact: Carol Shea
(413) 562-5147 Fax: (413) 568-2800
Gift store specializing in imported hand-knits, jewelry and woolen products. Tapes, films and Irish food products also available.

Irish Castle Imports Limited
6 Mount Vernon Street, #195
Winchester, MA 01890
Contact: Gerry Dunleavy
(617) 729-6563 Fax: (617) 721-4659
Importers of fine hand-crafts from various Irish artists with an aim to provide unique Irish products to the American market.

The Irish Connection
139 Massachusetts Avenue
Arlington, MA 02174
Contact: Patricia Higgins
(617) 641-3636

The Irish Cottage
21 Ledin Drive
Avon, MA 02322
Contact: Jim Mulligan
(617) 963-8203 Fax: (508) 559-6929
North America's largest Irish specialty retailer. See also New Hampshire and Rhode Island.

The Irish Cottage
South Shore Plaza
Braintree, MA 02184
(617) 848-8609

The Irish Cottage
Burlington Mall
Burlington, MA 01803
(617) 272-1044

The Irish Cottage
Dedham Mall
VFW Parkway
Dedham, MA 02026
(617) 326-6525

The Irish Cottage
1775 Washington Street
Hanover, MA 02339
(617) 829-0098

The Irish Cottage
North Shore Shopping Center
Peabody, MA 01960
(508) 531-1223

The Irish Cottage Import Gift Store
16 Apollo Road
Worcester, MA 01605
(508) 568-1707

Irish Crystal Company
129 Newbury Street
Boston, MA 02116
Contact: Martina Bromley-Kerr
(617) 536-1328 Fax: (617) 536-1457
Exquisite Irish crystal from Co. Tyrone.

Irish Imports Ltd.
1735 Massachusetts Avenue
Cambridge, MA 02138
(617) 354-2511
A colorful blend of Irish crafts, traditional and contemporary, soft woolens and crisp linens, rugged hand-knits and cozy blankets. Books, CD's and other hand-made arts and crafts are also available.

MASSACHUSETTS

Irish Items
821 Route 6A
Dennis on Cape Cod, MA 02638
(508) 358-9231

Irish Jaunting Car Imports
89 South Broadway
Lawrence, MA 01843
Contact: Dave Burke
(508) 683-9007

Irish Specialty Shop, Inc.
Executive Plaza
101 President Avenue
Fall River, MA 02720
Contact: Joseph Reilly/Mary Reilly
(508) 678-4096
A complete selection of gifts and clothing from Ireland including, Waterford Crystal, Claddagh Jewelry, Belleek China and Royal Tara China.

The Lucky Leprechaun, Inc.
114 Water Street
Plymouth, MA 02360
Contact: Dan Kelley
(508) 747-4030

The Moriartys
11 Gary Drive
Holyoke, MA 01040
Contact: Ed Moriarty/Pat Moriarty
(413) 532-8971 Fax: (413) 532-2012
Full range of quality Irish imports with special emphasis on better quality products considered top of the line.

Purple Heather
Pickering Wharf
Salem, MA 01970
(508) 744-6880

An Siopa Éireannach
310 Washington Street
Brighton, MA 02135
Contact: Frances Connolly
(617) 789-4222
Located near Brighton Center next to The Green Briar, Frances Connolly's, An Siopa Éireannach, carries a wide selec-tion of Irish clothes, giftware, jewelry, music and other Irish-made products.

The Tinker's Cart
7 Hillside Avenue
Clinton, MA 01510
Contact: John Hughes/Jane Hughes
(508) 365-4334 Fax: (508) 365-4769
Custom embroidery, specializing in Irish designs, serving restaurants, bars, sporting teams and other businesses.

Touch of Irish
133 Middlesex Avenue
Somerville, MA 02145
(617) 666-3411

Wolfhound Imports
21 Main Street
Nantucket, MA 02554
(508) 228-3552

World Soccer Shop
Faneuil Hall Marketplace
Boston, MA 02108
Contact: Tony Nugent
(617) 245-9696

Government Agencies

Consulate General of Ireland
535 Boylston Street
Boston, MA 02116
Contact: Consul General,
Conor O'Riordan
Contact: Vice-Consul General,
Ciarán Byrne
(617) 267-9330
The functions of the Consulate General may be broadly divided into two parts. The first is to provide a service to Irish citizens, which includes the issue of renewal of Irish passports, the processing of legal documents relating to property, the granting of Irish citizenship and advising Irish citizens in cases of unforeseen difficulties and emergencies. The second is the promotion of Irish interest in New England including the promotion of Ireland's political and economic interest and the dissemination of information on all aspects of Irish life.

Industrial Development Authority (IDA)
Three Center Plaza
Boston, MA 02108
(617) 367-8225
The IDA is the agency responsible for the development and implementation of the Irish Government's industrial and investment programs. It offers an attractive range of financial and other incentives to attract high quality mobile investment to Ireland.

Law Offices

Aidan Browne
Sullivan and Worcester
1 Post Office Square
Boston, MA 02109
(617) 338-2800

Camilla Duffy, Esq.
Dorchester, MA
(617) 287-9343
Litigation attorney including international law.

Flynn & Nyhan
Law Partnership
285 Washington Street
Braintree, MA 02184
Contact: Jack Nyhan, Esq.
Margaret Flynn, (B.A.L.L.B.)
Immigration and real estate.

Brian O'Neill
2 Financial Center
Boston, MA
(617) 722-4000
Specialists in immigration law.

Quinn & Morris
141 Tremont Street
Temple Place
Boston, MA 02108
Contact: Robert Quinn
(617) 423-3500
Attorney at law.

MONUMENTS

Celtic Monument Co.
22 Parkwood Drive
Milton, MA 02186
Contact: Paul Trapey Pils
(617) 383-2655

Milton Monument Co., Inc.
1060 North Main Street
Randolph, MA 02368
Contact: Mary Ellen Mulligan
(617) 963-3660 Fax: (617) 986-8004
Custom monuments, cemetery lettering and bronze markers. Quality service and low, low prices.

NEWSPAPERS

Adams Corner General Store
776 Adams Street, Adams Village
Dorchester, MA 02125
(617) 282-6370
Irish newspapers, candies and food products.

Conlon's Market
Ashmont Street
Dorchester, MA 02125
Contact: John Flaherty
Irish newspapers and food products.

McGowan's Corner Store
1658 Dorchester Avenue
Dorchester, MA 02122
Contact: Bill McGowan
(617) 265-9545
Irish newspapers, food products and meats.

Out of Town News
Harvard Square
Cambridge, MA 02138
Contact: Jim Finn
(617) 354-7777
Newspapers and magazines from all over the world including most of the Irish newspapers. County and Weekly magazines as well as Irish-American news.

Palace Spa
419 Washington Street
Brighton, MA 02135
(617) 787-1665
Irish newspapers.

Steve Slyne's Deli
1882 Centre Street
West Roxbury, MA 02132
Contact: Mike Slyne
(617) 325-0754
Imported Irish products and newspapers.

PHOTOGRAPHERS

Bill Brett
(617) 436-1222

Leslie Anne Feagley
1368 Commonwealth Avenue, #10
Allston, MA 02134
(617) 277-7075
Photographs of Irish scenes and graphic design services.

Brian Giltinan
(617) 325-4054

Jim Higgins
281 Princeton Street
North Chelmsford, MA 01863
(508) 454-4248

Bill McCormack
10 Eulita Terrace
Brighton, MA 02135
(617) 254-5011

John Redmond
8 Harris Street
Boston, MA 02109
(617) 367-6849

Bill Tonra
15 Grant Place
Dorchester, MA 02124
(617) 298-8533

Publishers

Boston Irish Reporter
305 Neponset Avenue
Dorchester, MA 02122
(617) 436-1222
Contact: Ed Forry, Publisher
Contact: Sue Asci, Editor
Boston's local Irish newspaper, covering events, activities and news of greater Boston's Irish community.

Folk Directory
PO Box 380867
Cambridge, MA 02238
Contact: Stephen Baird
(617) 522-3407 Fax: (617) 522-3407
Comprehensive guide to greater Boston and New England arts community. This 160 page directory lists festivals, clubs and coffee houses, radio programs and publications, dances and craft resources, teachers and artists for a total cost of $15.00.

Ford and Bailie Publishers/ Distributors
PO Box 138
Belmont, MA 02178
Contact: Chadine Bailie
(617) 489-6635 Fax: (617) 489-6388
Celtic books for scholars and students.

Irish World
217 St. Paul Street
Brookline, MA 02146
Contact: Michael Simpson
(617) 739-8540 Fax: (617) 232-4994
Irish World is an Irish organization which is now in Boston to help Irish-Americans trace their ancestry. They provide the most accurate service available as they have over five million records on computer data base.

New England Folk Almanac
PO Box 336
Cambridge, MA 02141
Contact: Scott Alarick
(617) 661-4708
Bi-monthly folk music chronicle and calendar. Reviews, features on friends and favorite performers, interviews, profiles with lots of photos. Calendar listings of over 1,000 events each issue.

Northeastern University Press
360 Huntington Avenue, 272HN
Boston, MA 02115
Contact: Jill Bachall
(617) 373-5481 Fax: (617) 373-5483
Publishers of "South Boston: My Home Town—The History of an Ethnic Neighborhood" and "Building a New Boston: Politics and Urban Renewal, 1950-1970," both by Thomas H. O'Connor, and "Eve Names the Animals" by Susan Donnelly. Available at bookstores.

Quinlin Campbell Publishers (QCP)
Post Office Box 651
Boston, MA 02134
Contact: Michael Quinlin
Contact: Colette Minogue
Tel/Fax: (617) 825-1404
Founded in 1979, QCP is publisher of The Guide To The New England Irish along with eight other publications including books on Irish music, Celtic language and politics. Currently working on a book of selected writings by John Boyle O'Reilly and a book on Irish music in Massachusetts.

Schooner Productions, Inc.
5 Bessem Street
Suite 101, Box 4000
Marblehead, MA 01945
Contact: Gary Kissal
(617) 631-2567
Dedicated to the writings of James Brendan Connolly, a South Boston native who won the first gold medal in the triple jump competition at the modern Olympics in 1896, and whose novels and stories of the sea made him one of the most popular writers of his time. Schooner Productions is seeking to establish a library of Connolly's papers and to commemorate his athletic accomplishments at the 1996 Olympics.

University of Massachusetts Press
Box 429
Amherst, MA 01004
Contact: Ralph Kaplan
(413) 545-2217 Fax: (413) 545-1226
Publishers of books on ethnicity in general and the experiences of the Irish-American in particular. Also publishers of books on Irish literature.

Yellow Moon Press
Box 1316
Cambridge, MA 02238
Contact: Brendan Robb
(617) 776-2230 (617) 776-8246
Distributors of author/story teller Maggi Peirce's books including "Maggi Peirce Live" and "An Ulster Christmas."

REAL ESTATE

Geraghty Associates, Inc.
45 Sierra Road
Readville, MA 02137
Contact: Margaret Geraghty
(617) 364-4000
Property management.

Alan & Una Loughnane Real Estate
14 Centre Street
Cambridge, MA 02139
(617) 876-1568
Sales, market analysis, consultancy and referrals. Personal service provided for all areas.

Moy Realty
382 Washington Street
Brookline, MA 02146
Contact: Mick Griffin
(617) 739-7226
Mayo-born Mick Griffin will help you purchase your home. For free consultation regarding purchase and sales, refinancing or construction financing, please call for an appointment.

Shipping Services

Allworld Removals Ltd.
434 Chelsea Street
East Boston, MA 02128
Contact: Gayle Fuller
(617) 569-0696 Fax: (617) 569-5689
International freight forwarder, fully licensed and bonded by the Federal Maritime Commission, specializing in the movement of automobiles and household items from New England worldwide.

Bill Black Agency
208 Worcester Court
Falmouth, MA 02540
Contact: Bill Black
(508) 540-6899

Tara Shipping & Trading, Inc.
460 Main Street, Unit 6
Wilmington, MA 01887
Contact: John Fitzpatrick
(508) 694-1022 (508) 694-9221
Fax: (508) 694-1519
100% Irish company with door-to-door service. Freight forwarders of both sea and air freight. Free estimates, no hidden charges, FMC bonded. They also have an office in Dublin, Ireland.

Travel Agencies

Concept Tours & Conferences
15 Depot Square
Lexington, MA 02173
Contact: Susan Burke
(617) 674-0137 Fax: (617) 674-2080
Concept Tours & Conferences, in association with Kátlin Travel Group, designs fine-tuned, tailored in-depth trips and/or conferences for business trade organizations and cultural and social groups.

County Travel & Tours
172 State Street
Newburyport, MA 01950
Contact: Terry Monahan
1-800-222-8283 Fax: (508) 465-5334
County Travel & Tours offers Irish travel specialists advice north of Boston. They provide a comprehensive service for all aspects of Irish travel.

Crystal Travel & Tours, Inc.
100 Spring Street
West Roxbury, MA 02132
Contact: Jim Kelly
1-800-327-3780
(617) 327-4242 Fax: (617) 327-7814
Largest travel agency in the United States specializing in travel to Ireland.

Erin World Travel
174 Elm Street
Westfield, MA 01085
Contact: Carol Shea
(413) 562-5147 Fax: (413) 568-2800
Travel agency specializing in land tours and tours to Ireland.

MASSACHUSETTS

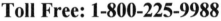

SERVICES

S E R V I C E S

Event and Travel Management LTD.
Tralee, County Kerry
3536623733
3536623389 (fax)
EMT offers unforgettable golfing holidays on Ireland's greatest courses.

Evergreen Travel
8 Chestnut Hill Avenue
Brighton, MA 02135
Contact: Mike Landers
(617) 254-0012
A full service travel agency, specializing in leisure travel worldwide.

Evergreen Travel
1401 Centre Street
Boston 02131
Contact: Mike Landers
(617) 469-5500
A full service travel agency, specializing in leisure travel worldwide.

Galway Bay Cottages
725 Plain Street
Marshfield, MA 02050
Contact: William McDonough
(617) 837-4405
Panoramic views overlooking Galway Bay. All cottages have three bedrooms with electric kitchen, color TV and videos.

Kátlin Travel Group
15 Depot Square
Lexington, MA 02173
Contact: Kathleen Kearney
(617) 862-6229 Fax: (617) 674-2080
A full service travel agency, specializing in leisure, corporate, group, incentive and special interest travel worldwide. Kátlin's agents offer a great deal of experience with Ireland as a destination.

O'Byrne DeWitt Travel
1751 Centre Street
West Roxbury, MA 02132
Contact: M. Eleanor Logan
(617) 325-5900 Fax: (617) 325-0160
Travel agency specializing in Ireland and England.

Noel Henry Tours
PO Box 91
Kingston, MA 02364
(617) 934-2200
(617) 934- 5708 (fax)
Musical tours of Ireland, cruises, getaway weekends and bus trips escorted by Noel Henry and his Showband.

Round Tower Travel
18 Central Street
Norwood, MA 02060
Contact: John Curran
(617) 762-9090
1-800-225-9988
Worldwide travel service for groups and corporate travelers. Authorized agency for Aer Lingus and all scheduled airlines. Tours, cruises, hotel reservations, car rentals, rail services and bus tours.

Sterling Travel
Shamrock Division
16 Brookside Avenue
Lexington, MA 02173
Contact: Joan Wall/Richard Williamson
1-800-873-4433
(617) 862-3434 Fax: (617) 861-3912
Low-cost premium travel, primarily to Ireland, the British Isles, Europe and other world-wide destinations.

Warehouse Services

Port Terminals Co., Inc.
17 Black Falcon Avenue
South Boston, MA 02210
Contact: Philip Hatfield
(617) 542-4500
Located in the Boston Marine Industrial Park, Port Terminals is the only warehouse/distribution facility on Boston Harbor. They have over 30 years of experience and 800,000 square foot storage space, currently storing over one million books for publishers. They charge $.20 to $.50 per foot per month for space in a certified bonded secured public warehouse.

Wholesalers

Irish Dancers Catalog
1-800-222-2088

Irish Imports Co.
Subsidiary of Irish J. C. Imports
89 South Broadway
Lawrence, MA 01843
(617) 689-9007

Wolfhound Manufacturing
60 Greenwood Avenue
Hyde Park, MA 02136
Contact: Uinseann MacCorascaigh
(617) 364-9618
Irish county sporting clothes, jackets, hats, rugby shirts in county colors.

Other

Aisling Flower Shop
703 Center Street
Jamaica Plain, MA 02130
Contact: Eileen Dunn
(617) 524-7970

Minihane's Flower & Garden Shop
425 Washington Street
Brighton, MA 02135
(617) 254-1130
Seasonal flowers available year 'round.

Sports

Currach Rowing Clubs

Boston Irish Currach Rowing Club
Contact: Johnny Joyce
(617) 265-7718

Gaelic Games

Gaelic Athletic Association
New England Division
c/o 151 Minot Street
Dorchester, MA 02122
Contact: Joe Lydon, President
(617) 282-5998
Maureen Doherty, Publicity Director
(617) 628-2438
The GAA was formed in 1884 to revive, cultivate and preserve Irish games and pastimes. It caught on rapidly and helped spawn a renaissance of interest in Irish literature, music, dancing and language. It helped to define a nationalistic pride in Ireland that had been damaged during the 19th century by the famine and immigration. Boston was the first city outside of Ireland to hold a match under GAA rules, in 1886. The Massachusetts GAA was officially formed in 1923 and since then has been active in promoting a high standard of Gaelic football, hurling, and camogie. Today the New England Board is the largest of ten North American divisions, and is responsible for organizing, scheduling and promoting these ancient Irish games.

Boston Shamrocks
c/o 183 Centre Street
Dorchester, MA 02125
Contact: Joan O'Connor
(617) 436-9767

Celtics Gaelic Football Club
c/o The Castlebar
575 Washington Street
Brighton, MA 02135
Contact: Séamus Maunsell
(617) 666-3105

Christopher's Football Club
107 Providence Street
Hyde Park, MA 02136
Contact: Noel Keane
(617) 469-2593

Connemara Gaels Football Club
6 Rosselerin Road
Dorchester, MA 02122
Contact: Gabriel Mannion
(617) 265-6727

Cork Football Club
26 Maitland Road
Milton, MA 02186
Contact: Debbie Delaney
(617) 288-7861

Cork Hurling Club
33 Chapman Street
Watertown, MA
Contact: Richard Moxley
(617) 924-2867

Donegal Gaelic Football Club
c/o McDevitt
183 Center Street
Dorchester, MA 02124
Contact: Maureen Doherty
(617) 628-2438

Father Tom Burke's Hurling Club
143 Nahanton Avenue
Milton, MA 02186
Contact: Pat Costello
(617) 698-7151

Galway Football Club
19 Ames Avenue
Canton, MA 02021
Contact: Gerry Meehan
(617) 828-6181

Galway Hurling Club
516 Washington Street
Brighton, MA 02135
Contact: Brian Glynn
(617) 254-8935

Kerry Gaelic Football Club
1156 Dorchester Avenue
Dorchester, MA
Contact: Robbie Griffin
(617) 825-3179

Mayo Football Club
23 Mt. Vernon Street
West Roxbury, MA 02132
Contact: Oliver Dempsey
(617) 361-0307

Notre Dame Irish Football Club
18 Foster Street
Brighton, MA 02135
Contact: John McDevitt
(617) 254-0187

Shannon Blues Gaelic Football Club
40 Worley Street
West Roxbury, MA 02132
Contact: Ollie Keegan
(617) 327-1952

Springfield Gaelic Football Club
20 Greaney Street
Springfield, MA 01104
Contact: Joe Campbell
(413) 739-7563

St. Columbkilles Football Club
c/o 57 South Crescent Circuit
Brighton, MA 02135
Contact: Terese Brosnan
(617) 783-0725

St. Patrick's Football Club
52 Cerdan Avenue
West Roxbury, MA 02132
Contact: Mike O'Connor
(617) 327-3071

Tipperary Hurling Club
105 School Street
Somerville, MA 02143
Contact: Sean Kennedy
(617) 628-2945

Wolfe Tones Gaelic Football Club
471 West Broadway
South Boston, MA 02127
Contact: Margaret Doherty
(617) 268-8809

Running

Irish Spring Shamrock Classic 5K Run
Dartmouth Street
Boston, MA
Contact: Sue Smith
(508) 655-6270
This popular road race, held the first Sunday in March, benefits Boston's Camp Joy program for disabled children. Prizes for men's, women's, seniors, wheelchair and children's races.

James Joyce Ramble
Contact: Martin Hanley
(617) 329-9744
A 10K roadrace held the last Sunday of April, where over 2,000 runners are cheered on by Joycean characters along the sidelines.

Malden Irish-American Road Races
177 West Street
Malden, MA 02148
Contact: Billy Kelly
(617) 324-9733
Held each Labor Day, the 5 and 10K races raise funds for local charities. The race begins in front of the Irish-American Club in Malden.

St. Patrick's Day 10K
Broadway Station
W. Broadway
South Boston, MA 02127
Contact: Ed Hoell
Held the same morning as the South Boston Parade, this Irish race along the coast, draws hundreds of contestants.

Other

Boston Irish Youth Boxing Club
3 Roseland Street
Dorchester, MA 02124
Contact: Yvonne Grealish
(617) 265-5954
A team of Boston youths who travel to Ireland for boxing matches, and who host Irish teams coming to Boston.

Irish Supporters Soccer Club
c/o The Kells
161 Brighton Avenue
Allston, MA 02134
Contact: Leo Cunningham/Tom Carty
(617) 782-6172
Avid supporters of the Irish Soccer Team gather here to cheer their team on and to arrange trips to watch the matches.

IN MEMORY OF BOSTON IRISH MUSICIANS

BILLY CAPLES
JOHNNY CRONIN
DANIEL CULLITY
JOHN HARTIGAN
MARY IRWIN
MARTIN MCDONAGH
FRANK NEYLON
NEAL NOLAN
GENE PRESTON
JOE RICHARDS
GEORGE SHANLEY

HANAFIN-COOLEY BRANCH
COMHALTAS CEOLTOIRI EIREANN
LARRY AND PHYLLIS REYNOLDS

New Hampshire's population: 1,109,252
New Hampshire's Irish population: 232,418

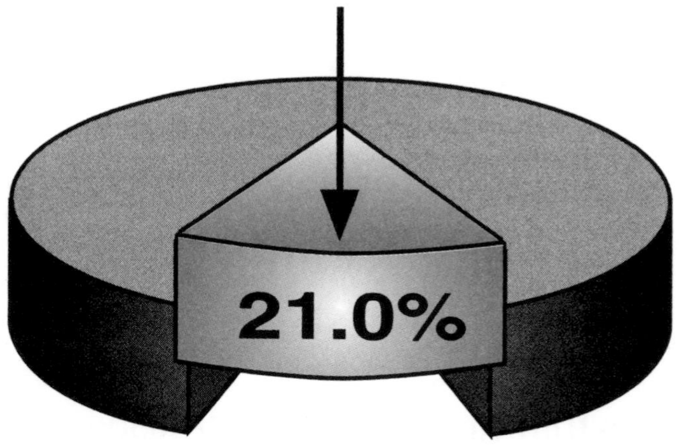

Annual Events

FEISEANNA

For Feis information or to register a Feis, write to: Mrs. Patricia Dwyer, President, North American Feis Commission (NAFC), 17 Lillburn Drive, Stony Point, New York 10980.

May
New Hampshire Feis
Contact: Rita O'Shea-Chaplin
(617) 665-3110

FESTIVALS

March
St. Patrick's Day Party and Annual Road Race
AOH of New Hampshire
Bedford, NH 03110
Contact: Richard Walsh
(603) 472-7355

Artisans

CELTIC ART/ART

Marcel Dion
(603) 666-0806
Celtic artwork, custom design.

Gallowglass Studio
4 Greenlay Street
Nashua, NH 03063
Contact: Arthur W. Ketchen
(603) 880-3706
Gallowglass is a consortium of artists led by Mr. Ketchen, who engage in a variaty of artistic mediums with Celtic themes including print making, painting, calligraphy and illustrations.

Institute of Celtic Studies East
800 Park Avenue, Suite 109
Keene, NH 03431
Contact: Jean McKeown
(617) 524-4386
Nonprofit group dedicated to the study, promotion and preservation of the Celtic cultural heritage of Ireland, Scotland, Wales, Cornwall, Brittany and the Isle of Mann, through literature, language, music and art.

Kevin Mulligan
21 Miami Street
Nashua, NH 03060-2538
(603) 883-4777
Fine art, landscapes, portraits in all mediums: watercolors, oils, acrylic, pencil, pen and ink. Murals for restaurants, pubs and homes.

OTHER

Tom O'Flaherty
RFD 6, Box 153
Lanconia, NH 03246
(603) 528-5733
Tom O'Flaherty lectures on Seán O'Flaherty, his grand-uncle, considered the master of the Irish short story.

Education

COLLEGES & UNIVERSITIES

Colby Sawyer College
New London, NH 03257
Contact: Patrick Anderson
(603) 526-2010 Ext. 3639
Humanities Dept.
Irish literature is offered as an independent study. Undergraduate courses are available on Anglo-Irish writers.

Dartmouth College
Hanover, NH 03755
(603) 646-1110 - English Dept.
Courses available on James Joyce.

Keene State College
Keene, NH 03431
Contact: Lindy Coggeshall
(603) 352-1909
Courses on Joyce, Yeats, Irish mythology and sagas. Exchange program with St. Patrick's College, Maynooth, Ireland.

Notre Dame College
Manchester, NH 03104
(603) 669-4298 - English Dept.
Courses available on the Irish Renaissance.

St. Anselm College
Manchester, NH 03104
(603) 641-7000 - History Dept.
Courses on the American Catholic Church and immigrant American history.

University of New Hampshire
Durham, NH 03824
Contact: W. R. Jones
(603) 862-1764 - History Dept.
Undergraduate courses in Irish history and literature.

University System of New Hampshire
School for Lifelong Learning
Berlin, NH 03570
Contact: Bernard Keenan
(603) 752-4224
Undergraduate and graduate course credits for teachers interested in studying education in Ireland. Courses offered at University College Galway or Queens University, Belfast. Call for free brochure.

Music/Dance

Bands & Performers

Roger Burridge
Locke Hill Road
Box 36F RFDI
Epsom, NH 02324
(603) 736-8650
One of the premier Irish fiddlers in New England, in great demand as a performer, session musician and teacher.

Eugene Byrne
6 Crestview Drive
Dover, NH 03820
(603) 742-0148
Experienced Irish folk singer in the New England area.

Kevin Byrne
6 Crestview Drive
Dover, NH 03820
(603) 742-0148
Irish and contemporary folk music.

Celtic Vision
4 Greenlay Street
Nashua, NH 03063
Contact: Art Ketchen
(603) 880-3706
Represents a wide range of Celtic musical expression from harpists to balladeers to the region's all women pipe band.

Tommy Makem
2 Longmeadow Road
Dover, NH 03820
Contact: Kevin O'Shea
(603) 742-3880 Fax: (603) 742-4503
Renowned Irish folk singer Tommy Makem has been delighting audiences across the world with song, story and wit for generations.

New Moon Ensemble
c/o Ossian USA
RR8 Box 374
Loudon, NH 03301
Contact: Philbin Clarke
(603) 783-4383 Fax: (603) 783-9660
Traditional and contemporary Celtic songs and instrumental works. New composition in the traditional style. Great flute, whistle, guitar, mandolin, fiddle and banjo with fine singing and vocal arrangements.

Marty Quirk
Oaklee Music
PO Box 3901
Manchester, NH 03105-3901
(603) 641-2536
Irish and original songs.

Tom Sweeney
2 Longmeadow Road
Dover, NH 03820
Contact: Tim Boucher
(603) 743-3569
Specializes in Irish music (guitar and whistle) and stories for children.

Ryan Thomson
c/o Celtic Vision
Contact: Art Ketchen
(603) 880-3706
Irish, Scottish, Welsh and Cajun fiddle and accordion.

Dancing

Merrimack Valley Set Dancers
Wheeler Dane Road
Salem, NH
Set dance and ceili dance lessons held on Thursday evenings. Monthly dance held at VFW Hall, Route 133, Georgetown, MA.

New Hampshire Feis
Contact: Rita O'Shea-Chaplin
(617) 665-3110

Tapes & CD's

KD Unlimited
PO Box 336
Dover, NH 03820-0336
Contact: Tim Boucher
Orders: (800) 27 Tunes
Inquiries: (603) 749-1263
Fax: (603) 742-4503
Tapes, CD's, videos and books from Tommy Makem, Barley Bree, Tom Sweeney, Brian Sullivan, Danny Quinn and the Clancy Brothers.

Ossian USA
RR8, Box 374
Loudon, NH 03301
Contact: Mary Lou Philbin and Charlie Clarke
(603) 783-4383 Fax: (603) 783-9660
A home-based business offering mail order sales of Irish music, sheet music, recordings and Irish traditional music books. Much of this material is unavailable from any other source in the USA.

Other

The House and Porch Concert Series
c/o RR8 Box 374 Beck Road
Loudon, NH 03301
Contact: Mary Lou Philbin/ Charlie Clarke
(603) 783-4383 Fax: (603) 783-9660
The House and Porch monthly concert series features regional acoustic musicians, especially those who sing and play traditional Celtic and American music. These concerts help benefit Between, a program which gives Northern Irish children and families a holiday in the US free from strife.

Between

c/o RR8
Box 374
Beck Road
Loudon, NH
03301

Between is a non-political, anti-sectarian, friendship society. Established in 1971, it has hosted over 9,000 people, bringing disadvantaged children from both Northern Ireland and the Republic of Ireland for a respite from strife at its Holiday Centre in County Cork.

For more information please call
Mary Lou Philbin and Charlie Clarke
(603) 783-4383
(603) 783-9660 (fax)

Organizations

Businesses Investments

Metropolitan Insurance Co.
24 Chestnut Street
Dover, NH 03820
Contact: Timothy Boucher
(603) 742-3422 Fax: (603) 742-2411
Life, health, accident, retirement, home and auto insurance available.

Philanthropy

Between
c/o RR8 Box 374 Beck Road
Loudon, NH 03301
Contact: Mary Lou Philbin/
Charlie Clarke
(603) 783-4383 Fax: (603) 783-9660
The Between program, based in Cork, is an effort to give Northern Irish children and families a holiday from strife. The House and Porch monthly concert series has been established to raise funds.

Social Clubs

Ancient Oder of Hibernians
The AOH was organized on May 4, 1836 in New York City. It played a pivotal role in helping Irish immigrants adjust to American society during the 19th century. Today the men's and women's branches of the AOH are active across the country promoting Irish culture, contributing to American values, Christian charity, the Catholic Church, supporting issues in Ireland and Northern Ireland and promoting friendship and unity within the organization.

State President
Richard Walsh
30 Birchwood Circle
Bedford, NH 03110
(603) 472-7355

Pubs/ Restaurants

Pubs

Claddagh Restaurant
168 1/2 Main Street
Nashua, NH 03060
Contact: Ann Tynann/Matt Tynann
(603) 889-3620
Irish and British food.

Rennaissance Coffeehouse
204 Main Street
Nashua, NH 03060
Contact: Tim Patarys
(603) 598-1890
Poetry readings, open mike, Celtic music and performing arts.

Shannon Door Pub
Route 16
Jackson, NH
(603) 383-4211
Irish music weekends.

Wild Rover Pub
21 Kosciuszko Street
Manchester, NH
(603) 669-7722
Singers Marty Quirk, Kevin Dolan and more.

OTHER

Shamrock Cruise Lines
18 Weirs Road
Gilford, NH
Contact: Walter Kelleher
(603) 293-3033
Serves lunch, dinner and Sunday brunch cruises on Lake Winnipesaukee on a magnificent 54 foot yacht, "The Ashling." Private charters from Weirs Beach dock also available.

Services

GIFT SHOPS

The Feis
Route 1, 862 Lafayette Road
North Hampton, NH 03860
(603) 926-2733

Irish Cottage of N.H., Inc.
Royal Ridge Mall
Nashua, NH 03060
(603) 888-4368

Irish Too
Main Street Marketplace
Hanover, NH 03755
(603) 643-3109

Scottish Lion Import Shop
Main Street
North Conway, NH 03860
(603) 356-5517

PUBLISHERS

Ossian USA Publications
RR8 Box 374 Beck Road
Loudon, NH 03301-9743
Contact: Mary Lou Philbin/
Charlie Clarke
(603) 783-4383 Fax: (603) 783-9660
Ossian USA Publications distributes a huge range of Irish music, including sheet music, songbooks, tune collections and instruction books. Catalogue available with Irish tape and CD listings.

TRAVEL SERVICES

Shamrock Cruise Lines
18 Weirs Road
Gilford, NH
Contact: Walter Kelleher
(603) 293-3033
Operates lunch, dinner and Sunday brunch cruises on Lake Winnipesaukee on "The Ashling," a magnificent 54 foot yacht. Private charters from Weirs Beach dock also available.

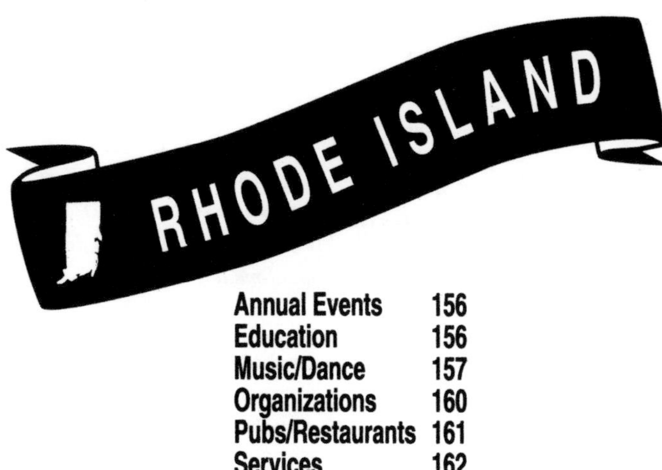

Rhode Island's population: 1,003,464
Rhode Island's Irish population: 213,684

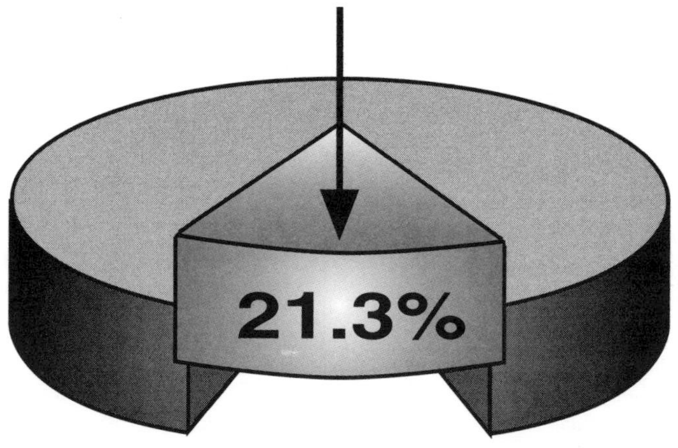

Annual Events

FEISEANNA

For Feis information or to register a Feis, write to: Mrs. Patricia Dwyer, President, North American Feis Commission (NAFC), 17 Lillburn Drive, Stony Point, New York 10980.

June
Newport Feis
Contact: Jack Milburn
(401) 847-2823

FESTIVALS

March
John Jameson's Road Race
(401) 849-0656
As part of Irish Heritage Month in Newport, this five mile road race, established in 1980, starts at Hibernian Hall on Wellington Avenue.

Newport Irish Heritage Association
PO Box 3114
Newport, RI 02840
Contact: Richard Kelly
(401) 846-6880
A non-profit organization dedicated to the preservation of Irish history and tradition. The NIHA coordinates Irish related events throughout the year including Newport Irish Heritage Month in March. Events include concerts, plays, films, exhibits and speaker programs.

Rhode Island Irish Festival
St. Patrick's School
Smith Street
Providence, RI
(401) 831-1856
Since 1984, the Providence Fest has featured outstanding regional and national traditional music, plus crafts workshops, set and ceili dancing and hand-made goods.

Rhode Island American and Irish Cultural Commission Exchange
47 Everett Street
Newport, RI 02840
Contact: Honorable Robert McKenna
(401) 846-9296 Fax: (401) 849-6923
The commission is the official state agency to promote Irish culture in Rhode Island.

Education

COLLEGES & UNIVERSITIES

Brown University
Providence, RI 02912
Contact: David Krause
(401) 863-2393 - English Dept.
Contact: Perry Curtis
(401) 863-2393 - History Dept.
Undergraduate and graduate courses in Irish literature. Yeats courses also available.

Providence College
Providence, RI 02918
Contact: Paul O'Malley
(401) 865-2193 - History Dept.
Undergraduate and graduate courses in Irish literature, history and politics.

Rhode Island College
Providence, RI 02908
Contact: James White
(401) 456-8027 - English Dept.
Undergraduate courses on ethnic groups in America.

Roger Williams University
Briston, RI 02809
(401) 253-1040 - History Dept.
Studies in national history, including Ireland.

Salve Regina College
Newport, RI 02840
Contact: Sr. Mary Concilia Reynolds
(401) 847-6650 - History Dept.
Undergraduate courses in Irish literature available.

University of Rhode Island
Kingston, RI 02881
Contact: Robert Lynch
(401) 792-2587 - Anthropology Dept.
Students can take minor in Irish studies by taking courses in anthropology, literature, Irish and theater.

Adult Education

Mance Grady
94 Angell Road
Cumberland, RI 02864
Contact: Lori Grady
(401) 333-2293
Ace bodhrán player, maker and teacher since 1977, available for group and/or private instruction on the bodhrán or bones.

Music/Dance

Bands & Performers

Atwater & Donnelly
(401) 826-3522
Traditional and original folk and Irish music on guitar, tinwhistle, banjo and vocals.

John Campbell
Uilleann pipes.

Bill Crozier
(401) 521-6181
Guitar, mandolin, and bouzouki.

Jimmy Devine
(401) 272-4402
Fiddle.

Fourin A Feire
Contact: Patrick Hutchinson
(401) 861-1577
Traditional music and song featuring fiddle, pipes, guitar and vocals.

Mance Grady
94 Angell Road
Cumberland, RI 02864
Contact: Lori Grady
(401) 333-2293
Ace bodhrán player, maker and teacher since 1977, available for group and/or private instruction on the bodhrán or bones, studio musician, guest performer, tailored workshops offered. Accompanist to storytellers, theater, dance and other artistic venues. Hand-crafted bodhráns and tippers (drumsticks) made from domestic and exotic woods are available with instructional videos.

Patrick Hutchinson
(401) 861-1577
Uilleann pipes.

Tina Lech
(401) 831-4897
Fiddle.

Barbara Lyons
(401) 732-4238
Fiddle.

Paul Mulvaney
Whistle and flute.

Christian Turner and Rachell Maloney
(401) 831-6208
Harmonica and fiddle.

Mark Roberts and Sandol Roberts
38 Wheaton Street
Warren, RI 02885
(401) 247-1654
Flute, five string banjoand vocals. Irish and old time music.

Teddi Scobi
(401) 751-7691
Flute and whistle.

Dancing

Deirdre Goulding
(401) 846-8519

Kathleen Hanley Perreault
85 Knowles Drive
Warwick, RI 02888
(401) 463-5153

Providence Ceili Club
Contact: Laura Travis
(401) 831-1856

Rhode Island Ceili Club
Contact: Frances McGuire

Radio Programs

WADK 1540 AM "Irish Hour"
Saturday's from 11:00 a.m. to Noon
140 Thames Street, Box 367
Newport, RI 02840
Contact: Rick Kelly
(401) 846-1540

WATD 95.9 FM
"Feast of Irish Music"
Sunday's from 9:30 a.m. to 12.30 p.m.

WICE 550 AM
"Irish Radio Program"
Sunday's from 9:00 a.m. to 10:00 a.m.
Contact: John Lyons
(401) 463-6012

WRIU 90.3 FM
"Celtic Realm"
Wednesdays from 7:00 p.m. to 9:00 p.m.
Contact: Sue Millard/Laura Travis
(401) 831-1856

Organizations

Political/Human Rights Groups

Irish Northern Aid
66 Daytona Avenue
Narragansett, RI 02882
Contact: Frank Murray
(401) 789-8690
INA is the oldest and largest organization in the US, dedicated exclusively to aiding the Nationalist victims of the Anglo-Irish conflict. The families of nearly 1,000 prisoners in five countries rely upon the dedication of volunteers to fund-raise across America on behalf of An Cuman Cabhrach and Green Cross, prisoner assisted trusts based in Ireland since the 1950's. INA works with Irish-Americans and human and civil rights groups to promote an end to conflict, to aid the release of prisoners, and to end British occupation of six counties in Ireland.

Social Clubs

Ancient Order of Hibernians
The AOH was organized on May 4, 1836 in New York City. It played a pivotal role in helping Irish immigrants adjust to American society during the 19th century. Today the men's and women's branches of the AOH are active across the country promoting Irish culture, contributing to American values, Christian charity, the Catholic Church, supporting issues in Ireland and Northern Ireland and promoting friendship and unity within the organization. The Rhode Island divisions are as follows:

State President
AOH - Division 2
John O'Connor
327 Spring Street
Newport, RI 02840
(401) 846-3357

AOH - Division 12
Paul McNeil
PO Box 945 Annex
Providence, RI 02901

Celtic Ceathair (Celtic Four)
310 Sayles Avenue
Pawtucket, RI 02869
Contact: Barbara Jencks
Group which meets monthly and on Irish feast days to discuss Irish events and history. Attend all Irish area events. Contribute to charitable projects in Rhode Island and in Ireland.

Friendly Sons of St. Patrick
623 Hospital Trust Building
Providence, RI 02903
Contact: Tom Sweeney
(401) 421-5350

OTHER

Newport Irish Heritage Association
PO Box 3114
Newport, RI 02840
Contact: Richard Kelly
(401) 846-6880
A non-profit organization dedicated to the preservation of Irish history and tradition. The NIHA coordinates Irish related events throughout the year including Newport Irish Heritage Month in March. Events include concerts, plays, films, exhibits and speaker programs.

Irish Heritage Month
Newport Irish Heritage Association
PO Box 3114
Newport, RI 02840
Contact: Richard Kelly
(401) 849-8048 1-800-458-4843
Formed in 1977 to celebrate Newport's Irish links, Heritage Month features a fall schedule of musical, cultural and educational programs, plus bread baking contests, a film series and lectures.

Pubs & Restaurants

PUBS

AS-220
115 Empire Street
Providence, RI 02912
(401) 831-9327
Rhode Island's premier arts centre features folk art, music and dance, including Celtic art and Irish sessions.

Harp and Shamrock
557 Warwick and Post Roads
Warwick, RI
(401) 467-8998
Features regular Irish musicians like Fintan Stanley, occasional sessions with Barbara Lyons.

Patrick's Pub
381 Smith Street
Providence, RI 02908
Contact: Patrick Griffin
(401) 751-1553
Live Irish music every Friday, Saturday and Sunday. Guinness, Harp and Bass on tap, pub grub available.

Services

Genealogy

Irish Roots, Inc.
3543 Pawtucket Avenue
Riverside, RI 02915
Contact: Charles Hall

Gift Shops

Ireland Calls
127 Swinburne Row
Newport, RI 02840
(401) 849-8174

The Irish Cottage
Garden City Center
150 Midway Road
Cranston, RI 02920
(401) 943-0282

Irish Imports Ltd.
Bowen's Wharf
Newport, RI 02840
(401) 847-3331

Irish Shop
Water Street
Block Island, RI 02807
(401) 466-2309

Moyarta
Bay Street
Watch Hill, RI 02891
(401) 596-4747

Thoroughbred Clothiers
150 Bellevue Avenue
Newport, RI 02840
(401) 848-7047

SERVICES

Vermont's population: 562,758
Vermont's Irish population: 100,847

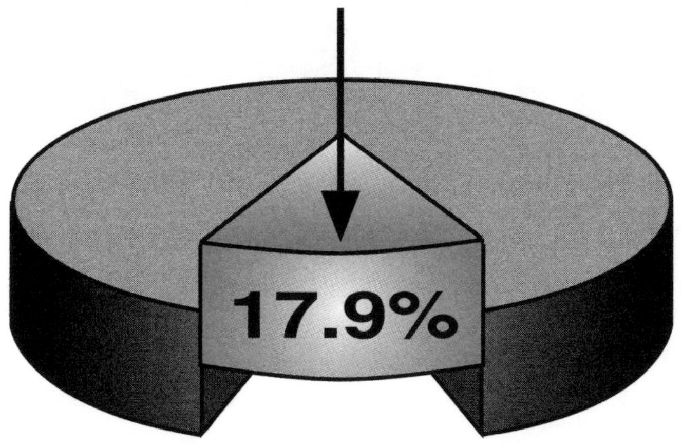

Annual Events

Festivals

Lake Champlain Festival
Box 163
Fairfax, VT 05454
Contact: Mark Sustic
(802) 849-6968 (802) 862-7771
This multi-musical festival features top Irish musicians like Séamus Connolly, Mick Maloney and others.

New World Festival
Contact: Tim Flynn
(802) 728-9823
Celtic and French-Canadian music Fest held in October.

Artisans

Celtic Art/Art

Simon Pearce Glass
The Mill
Quechee, VT 05059
(802) 295-2711
Handmade Irish glassware, using traditional techniques and materials following a family tradition. Catalogue available for $2.00.

Writing

Greg Delanty
380 South Winooski Avenue
Burlington, VT 05401
(802) 862-1259
Visiting Poet and lecturer at St. Michael's College, Winooski, VT, this Cork native is available for poetry readings and lectures.

Education

Colleges & Universities

Bennington College
Bennington, VT 05201
Contact: Dee Dee Heller
(802) 442-5401 - English Dept.
Courses available in Irish literature. Independent Irish studies also available.

Marlboro College
Marlboro, VT 05344
Contact: Timothy Little
(802) 257-4333 - History Dept.
Undergraduate courses on Yeats, Joyce and Irish history.

St. Michael's College
Winooski, VT 05404
Contact: Edward Murphy
(802) 655-2000 - English Dept.
Undergraduate courses in literature, poetry and politics available. Lecture series on Irish topics.

University of Vermont
Burlington, VT 05405
Contact: Anthony Bradley
(802) 656-3056 - English Dept.
Offers history and literature courses, plus numerous lectures, films and concerts.

Music/Dance

Bands/ Performers

Sarah Blair
RD #1, Box 3951
Worcester, VT 05682
(802) 223-0141 Fax: (802) 223-4826
Traditional Irish fiddler available for weddings, concerts and performances.

Eamonn Flynn
145A East Concord
Newingbury, VT
Fiddle and accordion.

Instrument Sales

Benedict Koehler
RFD 1 Box 9B
East Montpelier, VT 05651
(802) 223-4039
Accordion sales and repairs.

Music Lessons

Sarah Blair
RD #1, Box 3951
Worcester, VT 05682
(802) 223-0141 Fax: (802) 223-4826
Available for traditional Irish fiddle lessons.

Radio Programs

WRVT 88.7 FM
"Thistle & Shamrock"
4:00 p.m. - 5:00 p.m. - Sunday's
Contact: Fiona Ritchie
(704) 549-9323
A one hour syndicated program heard on 134 stations in the USA.

WVPR 89.5 FM
"Thistle & Shamrock"
4:00 p.m. - 5:00 p.m. - Sunday's
Contact: Fiona Ritchie
(704) 549-9323
A one hour syndicated program heard on 134 stations in the USA.

WVPS 107.9 FM
"Thistle & Shamrock"
4:00 p.m. - 5:00 p.m. - Sunday's
Contact: Fiona Ritchie
(704) 549-9323
A one hour syndicated program heard on 134 stations in the USA.

Organizations

Social Clubs

Ancient Order of Hibernians
The AOH was organized on May 4, 1836 in New York City. It played a pivotal role in helping Irish immigrants adjust to American society during the 19th century. Today the men's and women's branches of the AOH are active across the country promoting Irish culture, contributing to American values, Christian charity, the Catholic Church, supporting issues in Ireland and Northern Ireland and promoting friendship and unity within the organization.

State President
AOH - Division 1
E. Patrick Burke, Jr.
54 High Street
Proctor, VT 05765
(802) 773-3344

Project Children
Contact: Jim Carvey
(802) 483-6344
A national program to benefit Catholic and Protestant children from Northern Ireland who will visit the USA for a summer away from strife.

Pubs & Restaurants

Other

Inn at Long Trail
Route 4, PO 267
Killington, VT 05751
Contact: The McGrath Family
1-800-325-2540
This historic country inn/ski lodge features live Irish music weekends and serves traditional Irish fare.

Services

Gift Shops

Celtic Cottage Ltd.
Burlington Square Mall
Burlington, VT 05401
Contact: Verna Friedman
(802) 863-5524
Irish, Scottish and Welsh clothes, jewelry, books, music, prints, pottery, crystal and china.

The Irish House
Union Street
Manchester, VT 05254
(802) 362-4004

Simon Pearce Glass
The Mill
Quechee, VT 05059
Contact: Simon Pearce
(802) 295-2711
Mr. Pearce, a Cork native carries on a family tradition of making Irish glassware using traditional techniques and materials. Catalogue available.

Other

Information Ireland
Rutland, VT
(802) 773-8083
Keep in touch with news, sports, weather, current affairs and upcoming events by calling 1-900-420 Éire, 99¢ per minute.

D

E

L

M

N

O

P

ADVERTISERS

BOSTON IRISH HERITAGE TRAIL

History permeates Boston, reminding us that the past and present are merely a prelude to the future, an ongoing story waiting to be told and re-told. The Irish, who have settled in Boston since colonial times, relish history *and* storytelling, so it is fitting that a Boston Irish Heritage Trail present a portion of their tale.

These selected memorials evoke the memories of individuals and groups who helped enrich the Irish-American community and society at-large. Local educational institutions contributing to the Irish-American community are also included. Boston College and Harvard University are exceptional for the quality and breadth of their Irish Studies programs. Call these institutions for information on educational courses and for a schedule of public events. The Kennedy Library and Museum keeps alive the accomplishments of Boston's most famous Irish-American, and provides insight into the evolution of the Boston Irish. The Boston Public Library remains a veritable goldmine for scholars of Boston Irish history, and presents quality Irish lectures and films for the general public.

Plans are underway for a fuller depiction of the Irish-American contribution throughout the region. Please contact the publisher with suggestions about significant landmarks, individuals or historical passages relevant to the Irish-American experience in New England.

BOSTON IRISH

1 THE NEW MUSEUM AT THE JOHN F. KENNEDY LIBRARY

Harbor Point, Morrissey Blvd.
Dorchester, MA 02125
(617) 929-4523

As the first Irish Catholic President of the United States, John F. Kennedy signifies the triumph of the Irish in America. The presidential museum includes dramatic exhibits of Kennedy's political career, featuring re-creations of the Oval Office, interactive computers, historical documents, and Kennedy memorabilia, plus artifacts and a film on Kennedy's Irish ancestry and his visit to County Wexford in 1962.

Daily Hours: 9 a.m. to 5 p.m. (Admission varies)
MBTA: Red Line/JFK/U.Mass Station (Free shuttle to the Library)

2 JAMES BRENDAN CONNOLLY MEMORIAL

Columbus Park, Old Colony Road, South Boston

James Brendan Connolly, son of Irish immigrants, won the first gold medal in the modern Olympics in 1896, competing in the triple jump. Before his winning jump he shouted "This is for Galway." Connolly won medals in subsequent Olympic Games, then went on to become a prolific writer, producing 50 novels and 200 short stories about the sea. An effort is underway to commemorate his achievements at the 1996 Olympic Games in Atlanta.

Hours: Park is open daily until 11:00 p.m.
MBTA: Red Line/JFK/U.Mass Station, 3 minute walk to park.

3 ROSE KENNEDY GARDEN

Christopher Columbus Park, Atlantic Avenue
North End, Boston

Boston's North End was an Irish enclave in the late 19th century. Rose Fitzgerald Kennedy, the mother of President Kennedy, was born at nearby 4 Garden Court. City officials and local residents honored her with a Rose Garden overlooking Boston harbor.

Hours: Park is open daily until 11:00 p.m.
MBTA: Blue Line/Aquarium Station

4 GREAT HUNGER MEMORIAL

North Marketplace, Faneuil Hall, Boston

Commemorating the 150th anniversary of the Irish Famine, when thousands of Irish fled Ireland in the 1840s, to seek solace in America, this Memorial marks the spot where many immigrants first set foot in Boston. The memorial will be unveiled in 1995, as part of an international rememberance of the Irish Famine.

MBTA: Blue Line/Aquarium, cross Atlantic Avenue to Faneuil Hall.

5 JAMES MICHAEL CURLEY STATUES

Curley Park, Union Street, Boston

Curley dominated Boston politics for half a century, serving as mayor, governor, and congressman, plus two prison terms. A son of Galway immigrants, Curley was admired by working families who believed "his triumph was their triumph" while resented by opponents for his zealous railing against the establishment and his unorthodox political style.

Hours: Park is open until 11:00 p.m.
MBTA: Orange Line/Haymarket, walk toward Boston City Hall.

6 OLD GRANARY BURYING GROUNDS

Tremont Street, Boston (near Park Street Church)

The oldest burial ground in Boston (1660), the Granary contains numerous Irish heroes such as John Hancock, a signer of the Declaration of Independence, whose family emigrated from County Down in Northern Ireland. The Granary is the resting place of the five victims of the Boston Massacre (1770), including Irishman Patrick Carr.

Hours: 8:30 a.m. to 5:30 p.m. (Extended in summer months)
MBTA: Green Line/Park Street Station

7 COMMODORE JOHN BARRY MEMORIAL

Tremont Street, Boston Common
(Next to Visitors Information Center)

Born in Wexford in 1745, Barry was appointed by George Washington to "plan the construction of and later to be in command of the first U.S. Navy" launched in 1798. Barry is considered to be the Father of the American Navy. This memorial was dedicated in 1949 by Mayor Curley.

Hours: Park is open until 11:00 p.m.
MBTA: Green Line/Park Street Station

8 CENTRAL BURYING GROUND

Boylston Street at Tremont Street, Boston Common

Contains the earliest depictions of Celtic crosses in Boston's historic cemeteries. The markers are mostly from the early 1800s, and often mention the counties from which the Irish Catholic immigrants came. Created in 1758, the Central Burying Ground was traditionally the burying place for "strangers," those who died while visiting Boston, as well as Catholics and non-Protestant religious denominations.

Hours: 8:30 a.m. to 3:30 p.m.
MBTA: Green Line/Boylston, Theater District Station

9 THOMAS CASS MEMORIAL

Public Garden, Boylston Street near Arlington Street

Born in Queen's County (Laois) Ireland, Thomas Cass was a successful businessman and member of the Boston School Committee. When the Civil War began Massachusetts Governor Andrew asked Cass to form an Irish Regiment, the 9th Mass. Volunteers. Cass led the 9th Regiment, which fought bravely in the Civil War, and was himself mortally wounded at the Battle of Malvern Hill. He returned to Boston and died in 1862. In 1991 the Ancient Order of Hibernians established a maintenance endowment fund to preserve this memorial. Cass is buried at Mt. Auburn Cemetery in Cambridge.

MBTA: Green Line/Arlington Station

HERITAGE TRAIL

10 PATRICK COLLINS STATUE
Commonwealth Avenue Mall
(Between Clarendon and Dartmouth Streets)
Born in Fermoy, County Cork, Collins was the second Irish-born mayor in Boston's history (Hugh O'Brien, elected in 1884, was the first). After serving three years in office, Collins died in 1905. Funds for his memorial were raised in just six days by thousands of small contributions from Boston residents, a tribute to his enormous popularity.
Hours: the Mall is always open.
MBTA: Green Line/Copley Station. Follow Dartmouth to Commonwealth Avenue.

11 BOSTON PUBLIC LIBRARY
660 Boylston Street (at Dartmouth Street)
(617) 536-5400
Established in 1852, the BPL was the first free public library in the country. It was conceived in part because of the thousands of Irish immigrants pouring into Boston, most of them illiterate and poorly educated. The BPL was, and remains, "Free to All," and offers over 6 million books, including some excellent collections of Irish material dating from the 19th century.
Hours: 9:00 a.m. to 9:00 p.m. (Monday--Thursday), 9:00 a.m. to 5:00 p.m. (Friday and Saturday)
MBTA: Green Line/Copley

12 JOHN BOYLE O'REILLY MEMORIAL
Boylston and Fenway Streets
This legendary poet, patriot, and social reformer, born in Drogheda, exemplified the generation of Irish who combined passion for justice with democratic sensibility in late 19th century Boston. Imprisoned as a youth by Britain for crimes against the Crown, O'Reilly made a daring escape from an Australian prison and arrived in the United States, where he became editor of *The Pilot* and a spokesman for the Irish in America. He also defended the rights of Blacks, Jews, Chinese and other oppressed minorities at that time. When he died in 1892, he was praised by presidents, statesmen and ordinary people alike for his commitment to humanity.
MBTA: Green Line/Auditorium Station.

13 EUGENE O'NEILL GRAVESITE
Forest Hills Cemetery
Morton Street (Rt 203) Jamaica Plain, MA 02130
(617) 524-0128
Son of celebrated Irish actor James O'Neill, Eugene O'Neill (1888-1953) is considered one of the great playwrights. He was the only American to win the Nobel Prize for Literature, as well as four Pulitzer Prizes. His plays, *The Touch of the Poet* and *Moon for the Misbegotten*, helped to transform American drama from vaudville to a new realism. O'Neill spent his final years in Boston, battling Parkinson's Disease, in order to be near his doctor.
Hours:7: 00 a.m. to Dusk
MBTA: Orange Line/Forest Hills Station

14 JAMES MICHAEL CURLEY HOUSE
350 Jamaicaway, Jamaica Plain
Curley built this Georgian Revival 21 room mansion in 1915, complete with a crystal chandelier, Italian marble fireplace, mahogany interior and a three story spiral staircase, and overlooking Jamaica Pond. The ornate shamrocks carved into the 30 white window shutters came to symbolize Curley's ethnic politics and triumphalism. The mansion was purchased by the City of Boston in 1988 and is being used for youth Leadership conferences and community events.
Orange Line: Green Street Station

15 BOSTON COLLEGE IRISH STUDIES PROGRAM
Carney Hall, Irish Studies Office
Commonwealth Avenue, Chestnut Hill, 02167
(617) 552-3938
BC has the largest Irish Studies program in the United States. The college offers undergraduate and graduate degrees, lecture series, evening courses, study in Ireland, music and theater. It's excellent library facilities includes the Tip O'Neill Library. The Burns Library houses an Irish music archieves, the largest Yeats collection in the world, an expanded Beckett collection and other important Irish materials.
MBTA: Green Line/Boston College Station

16 HARVARD CELTIC STUDIES PROGRAM
Harvard University
61 Kirkland Street, Cambridge, MA 02138
(617) 495-1206
The Department of Celtic Languages has one of the best programs in the world dedicated to the scholarly pursuit of the Irish language. Advanced degrees are available. The Harvard Library has over 20,000 books in Celtic Studies, plus a considerable number of original manuscripts and facsimilies.
MBTA: Red Line/Harvard Station

17 FANNY PARNELL'S GRAVESITE
Mt. Auburn Cemetery
580 Mt. Auburn Street, Cambridge, MA 02138
(617) 547-7105
Sister of Charles Stuart Parnell, Fanny and her sister Anna were stalwarts in the Ladies Land League in the late 19th century, with chapters in Ireland, Canada and the United States. Poet, nationalist, and intellectual, Parnell made an enormous contribution to land reform and the Home Rule movement in Ireland. She is buried in the Tudor Lot in Mt. Auburn Cemetery. (Thomas Cass is also buried at Mt. Auburn Cemetery.)
Hours: 7:00 a.m. to Dusk
MBTA: Red Line/Harvard Station, Take #71 or 73 Bus up Mt. Auburn Avenue.